"From the first dramatic scene to the amazing denouement, Pat Piety's life story had me spellbound. I will never forget this unique memoir, with its honest revelations about a woman's life and times, by turns searingly tragic and richly ironic. Piety possesses a wicked sense of humor and an eye for the telling detail. A brilliant work."

~Meg Selig, Author and Blogger for PsychologyToday.com.

"Toward the end of this memoir, Piety writes, 'Every bad experience I've had and every mistake I've made has taught me something about how to love, appreciate, and empathize with my fellow human beings.' Readers of this memoir full of thoughtful reminiscences of Piety's fierce attachment to her parents, the intricacies of marriages, the stigma of abortion, and the inner workings of the Assemblies of God church will find themselves wrapped up in her memories but also reflecting on their own. Piety uses words the way a skilled surgeon wields a scalpel, leaving us more forgiving of ourselves and others."

~Patricia Macvaugh, Ed.D., Professor, English Department, Oklahoma State University

Don't Get Yourself Talked About

Don't Get Yourself Talked About

Pat Piety

Copyright © 2015 Pat Piety
All rights reserved.

ISBN: 1507846444
ISBN 13: 9781507846445

For my mother, my daughters, my grandmothers, and women everywhere.

The photo of the author on the cover was taken by her mother, Mary Ruth Chamless, on the beach in Rio de Janeiro, 1979.

Preface

I could never have written this book during my parents' lifetime. But I like to believe that on their deathbeds—or after dying, if there is an afterlife—people are inclined to forgive themselves and others for their human failings and less obsessed with the need for secrecy. I have always believed that the truth will make you free. I hope I'm right. I loved my parents with all my heart, I respect the many good things they did in rearing me, and I revere their memory. I hope that if they are looking down from somewhere, they will understand why I felt the need to tell our story.

"Don't get yourself talked about" is the advice my mother often gave me when I was growing up—advice that I was spectacularly bad at taking. In my previous book, *The Dance of Life: Perspectives*, I included one chapter titled "The Room: A Fragment," which tells about a traumatic event that happened on my fifteenth birthday that got me more talked about than either of us could ever have imagined. This book begins with "The Room" and then goes back to my early childhood and adolescence in an effort to examine how I got to that particular place on that fateful day. It also describes the immediate and long-term repercussions of that event for everyone in my immediate family. And finally, it shares a number of surprising revelations about it that cropped up over the next half century.

When we tell the story of our lives, we are always limited by the fallibility of memory, the vagaries of personal perspective, and our limitations as storytellers. Recognizing those limitations, I have tried to do justice to all the incidents and persons involved. I hope readers will find something in this book that will inspire more thoughtful discussion about some of the issues we all face in this complex web of human existence.

"For me remembrance is mostly taken up with acknowledgement of death. When my life fulfills its only precondition—its own ending—my memory will vanish. Nothing is being recorded, nobody is keeping score. Your childhood bedroom, your first kiss. They go with you. Better to think of memory as like food, or sex, or books: a reason to believe in the perishable days. A way to manage being alive."
Charles Finch
The Last Enchantments
St. Martin's Press, 2014

I thought I would never forget anything about that room. As I lay on the bed the night before my fifteenth birthday, I surveyed it like an archeologist, carefully noting everything: the perfectly smooth white woodwork and the shoulder-high windows that wrapped around the corner, covered by heavy drapes. But now I'm no longer sure about all the details—whether the walls were mint green or beige or the woodwork included fancy scrolled corners or plain miter joints. It was a very long time ago.

I can tell you that the door was opposite the foot of the bed, and I remember watching the doctor's wife coming through it and laying a tray of food on the rolling hospital table that stretched across my bed: a homemade hamburger on Wonder Bread, thick and juicy, but lightly seasoned, along with a glass of milk. "We don't want your stomach to be upset later on," she said.

Her husband had already placed the packing inside me, and she had given me a shot of Vitamin K, "to make sure your blood is clotting properly." There was no phone in the room, and cell phones were still a science fiction fantasy. I had been told that I could not make any calls, and if I wanted to use the toilet, I had to ring a bell for permission. It would be awkward, the doctor's wife explained, if I were to run into another girl in the hall. I had neglected to count the doors on the way in, so I had no idea how many other girls in my predicament might be moving through the house during the next few hours.

He was apparently a real doctor, because I could hear the voices of workmen in the basement addressing him as "doctor," and his wife seemed to be a nurse. The room where the doctor had filled me with packing and where the procedure would be performed much later that evening was fully equipped with table and stirrups, overhead lights, sink and a gas cone his wife would use to put me under ever so lightly. Through the buzz, I could feel something twisting and turning inside me and hear water running as he washed his hands afterwards.

Now that I know St. Louis better, I think the house was in Clayton or Ladue, since the doctor had picked me up outside the Clayton Famous-Barr department store, and we didn't drive very far. But I wasn't familiar with St. Louis suburbs back then, being from across the river, in Illinois. I had been instructed to stand alone by the curb and watch for a Cadillac with a monogram on the passenger-side door. I think the doctor's first name was Morris. His last name started with an "S." I remember what it was, but there are still several people in St. Louis with that name who are prominent donors to cultural institutions, and there's no reason to involve them in my story.

"When did you have your last period?" he asked as we drove away from the department store. When I told him, he slowed down and made a turn, heading back toward the place where he had picked me up. "You're farther along than I thought," he said. "You'll have to spend the night, and it will cost more. Do you think your parents have already left? I'll have to have their OK before I can go ahead with it."

"I don't know. It's just my dad. He said he was going to look around for a while. Maybe he's still there."

"See if you can find him, and tell him it's going to cost $400 instead of $200, and that you'll have to spend the night. I'll be back out front in 20 minutes."

Dad was in the book department—the first place I headed. Although he appreciated beautiful things, nothing material ever mattered much to him, except books. Often when I saw him tenderly hold an old leather-bound first edition and reverently turn its rag-paper pages, I thought I would be lucky if I ever found anything to love as much as he loved books.

Until a few days before, I had thought I loved Ronnie. Now I wasn't thinking at all, even though I was carrying his baby. On our way to Piggott, Arkansas, in his second-hand Pontiac, Ronnie had given me a wedding ring with a tiny chip diamond in it. We had heard there was no waiting period there, and that girls didn't have to be over 16 to get married without their parents' consent. I was prepared to lie about my age, but when we arrived, we found the rules had changed. There was a waiting period, and blood tests, and you needed a birth certificate. I had no idea where my birth certificate was, and we couldn't afford to stay in a motel three days. Anyway, I knew that within a few hours my parents would have the Highway Patrol after us. So we turned around and drove home through the night, stopping to make love in the car in Olive Branch, Illinois, not speaking about what was awaiting us at home.

That was a week before my night at the doctor's house—a week during which, in mute guilt and shame, I had surrendered my will to my parents. Mom seemed to be running the show, as usual. Dad was a mere shadow in the drama, the pick-up and delivery guy.

"Let me see your breasts," Mom said, after Ronnie had been banished and I put on my nightgown and crawled into bed. Unlike some of my friends' mothers, Mom never let me see her in her underwear, and she probably hadn't seen my naked body since I had learned to bathe myself, so being commanded to bare my breasts to her only intensified my sense of dream walking.

"That's what I was afraid of," she shook her head sadly when she saw my brown, distended nipples. The next day, she drove me to a doctor's office in East St. Louis, where her diagnosis was confirmed.

I refused to wear the white gown when the doctor examined me. If he was going to look at my most private parts, it seemed silly for me to cover up the rest of my body. He didn't argue. A kindly but haggard man with bags under his eyes, hair that fell down over one eye and cigarette smoke clinging to his white coat, he told me to put my clothes back on after he finished examining me and called my mother into the room.

"How many times have you had intercourse?" he asked. Mom shook her head sadly when I said I didn't know. He then sent me out of the room to talk to her privately, and a couple of days later I found myself a passenger in another doctor's car, heading toward a strange house in suburban St. Louis. There was an exotic, unfamiliar odor in the car, like I figured Turkish cigarettes might smell if I had ever smelled any.

I'm not sure I had any rational thoughts from the time Ronnie had dropped me off at my house until after everything was over. I must have read a book—I was always reading a book—but I can't remember it. If I missed Ronnie, I don't remember that, either.

It was 1954, and my parents were co-pastors of a tiny Assemblies of God church in East St. Louis, Illinois, a church that didn't believe in sex before marriage or divorce afterwards—and certainly not abortion at any time. Anyway, abortion was still illegal in the United States. If anyone ever found out what Mom and Dad were doing, they would not only lose their church, they would lose their licenses as ministers. And they would probably go to jail. They didn't have to tell me; I just knew.

I don't remember the conversation with Dad in the book department that night. All I know is that I found myself back in the doctor's car, riding along unfamiliar streets. We pulled into an attached garage and entered the house through the kitchen, where the doctor's wife, a friendly, middle-aged woman with black hair, greeted me and led me down a hall to my room. The room in which I lay waiting for the rest of my life to happen.

The repercussions from my fifteenth birthday have reverberated in many ways for the rest of my life. That is why I chose this pivotal point in my life to begin my story. The actual procedure went off smoothly, but I continued to feel numb to everything but shame and emptiness for several weeks. Although I can remember a lot of the details of that night in the doctor's private operating room, the weeks that followed are mostly a blur.

I remember one night feeling very sick, having a fever, and being struck by the look of terror on my mother's face. "She thinks I might die, and she doesn't know what to do," I thought. Another night, something—I have no idea what—sent me into a fit of full-blown hysteria, crying, screaming, and thrashing around. Under ordinary circumstances, I wouldn't have squealed over a mouse; Mother never allowed that kind of "silly" behavior. But that night when I lost control, Dad slapped my face. I remember thinking, "He's heard somewhere that slapping is what you do to people who get hysterical, but it's not working." In fact, his uncharacteristic behavior made me feel even more out of control.

A few days after I came home from St. Louis, Mom took me back to the doctor in East St. Louis who had confirmed my pregnancy and who must have been aware, all along, that it was going to be terminated. He gave me a clean bill of health and a note for the school nurse that didn't specify why I had been absent, simply telling me, "If she asks why you were out so long, just tell her it's none of her business." Looking back, I realize how terribly young I was at the time, because when I took the note in to the nurse upon my return to school after a two-week absence, she *did* ask, and, not knowing what else to say, I replied, "The doctor said to tell you it's none of your business." I guess I'm lucky she didn't throw me out, but she let me go without further discussion.

There was probably some gossip around Belleville Township High School, even though Ronnie lived in East St. Louis and hadn't attended high school in either city. I had been fairly involved in school activities during my freshman year, starring in one of the freshman one-act plays, playing the flute in the orchestra, and making all A's the first semester, so I wasn't entirely invisible, despite the fact that belonging to a church which didn't approve of dances or movies kept me from being fully integrated into the social activities of my classmates. A couple of girls in the school were members of our church, but they never asked me about why I had been out, although no doubt people were talking about it at church. I do remember a very wonderful and kindly man, Mr. Tabor, my geometry teacher, who helped me more than he will ever know. On my first day back, he asked me after class if I wanted to talk about why I had been out for two weeks. When I started to tear up, he waved his question away and let me go. The next day, when he was questioning the class about a theorem, I raised my hand to answer, and he said, "Look at Pat—she's been out two weeks and she knows more than the rest of you." It's teachers like him who save children's lives.

All the while, though, Ronnie was still out there; his widowed mother was a member of our church, and everyone in our little closed community would know that I had run away with him. Ronnie knew I had thought I was pregnant, so he would have questions, but I wasn't allowed to see him. If somehow he managed to get to me, I was to tell him that the pregnancy had been a false alarm, and I was not to admit to anyone that we had been intimate. I didn't tell my parents that I had long since shared that information with several girlfriends from church during some of our overnight visits.

Worst of all, I was struggling with some highly secret guilt feelings. Even though I was in love with Ronnie in a way that only adolescents can be, I knew that part of my motivation in having sex with him had been to get back at my mother for how I felt she had mistreated me for the past six years. And while I longed for Ronnie and grieved over what had happened, I also knew somewhere deep in my heart that I had felt more than a little ambivalence about getting married at fourteen and becoming a mother at fifteen. I had always assumed I would go to college and have a profession. A year or so before, I had tried to get Ronnie to finish high school through correspondence courses. I sent off for information in response to a magazine ad, and a representative from the school had called him, but he hadn't seemed interested. So, underneath everything else, I was aware of a certain relief, which only added to the burden of guilt that was destined to weigh more heavily as events continued to unfold.

For many years after that fateful event, I thought of myself as the victim of an unhappy childhood, but the more I dug into my memory, I had to admit that much of my childhood was extraordinarily happy—especially the early years. From birth to age 8, I enjoyed a life of unusual adventure and special attention. During that time, there were only three of us: my mother, Mary Ruth (Rainbolt) Chamless, my dad, Paul Vernon Chamless, and me—and it seemed to me that we were very happy. Now that both of my parents are gone, I often experience an intense loneliness because there is no one to share my memories of those days. My brother, John, didn't come along until I was almost nine years old, and for much of my adult life I wasn't consciously aware of the role my mother's pregnancy and his birth had played in my precocious sexual activity. But I am convinced that the situation was much more complicated than a simple case of sibling rivalry. For all I knew, I adored my baby brother. Even our mother freely admitted that I had been like a mother to him. But, for many reasons, the year leading up to his birth and the next few that followed constituted a period in which my whole world was turned upside down—and not just my world, but that of the whole family.

From the time I was 2½ until I started first grade in 1944, one month shy of 6 years old, Mom, Dad and I were virtual gypsies, on the road most of the time. They were evangelists and most of our travels took us to towns between my dad's home state of Texas and my mother's parents' home in downstate Illinois, across the Mississippi River from St. Louis. Although we did occasionally venture as far north as Michigan, west into New Mexico or east into Kentucky, Arkansas and Tennessee, for the most part we stayed near U.S. Route 66, traveling in our black Chevy coupe. During those years, I spent many happy hours napping on the crib mattress that was squeezed between the front and back seats or watching the world go by while singing long, meandering songs of my own composing. I especially loved driving through small towns at night, seeing the lighted windows of the houses and wondering what life was like inside.

Sometimes I would sit up front between Mom and Dad. Pretending that the radio grille was a piano and resting my foot lightly on the starter pedal on the floor to my left, I would accompany myself as I sang "You Are My Sunshine" or other songs my mother had taught me.

"Step on it Babe!" my dad once said in response to my lively playing. The sudden grinding when I pressed down on the starter pedal startled all three of us, but Daddy didn't scold me. He just explained that I shouldn't literally step on the "piano pedal." Often, my mother sang along with me during these musical road sessions, and perhaps that's how I learned to sing harmony before I started to school.

I'm sure it had to be hot and dirty riding in the car without air conditioning during the summer, but I don't remember being uncomfortable or hearing my parents complain. We didn't know anything else. On those long rides, we amused ourselves not only by singing and talking, but by reading the Burma Shave jingles spread out a phrase at a time on fences alongside the highway:

"Does your husband/misbehave/grunt and grumble/rant and rave?/ Shoot the brute some/Burma Shave."

Those Burma Shave signs may be how I learned to read. I know that my mother took every opportunity to educate me in my early childhood. She always claimed that my very first sentence startled her. Uttered in three parts, with long, dramatic pauses in between, it was, she claimed, "In a minute . . . I want . . . a drink of water." She also loved to tell about the time a woman tried to communicate with me in baby talk when I was around two years old. Turning to look up at my mother, I said, very distinctly and with genuine puzzlement, "What did she say?"

I don't remember those incidents, nor do I remember counting steps aloud with Mother when we climbed stairs, which she also told me that she had done. Many years later, when she was around 80 years old, she confessed that she had been an obsessive counter all her life. She said she had worked out a system for grouping windows in buildings so she could quickly count them all as we drove by on our frequent rides together. This was one of many symptoms of an extreme nervous ailment, probably a form of OCD, that would dog her throughout her life and often make life miserable for those around her.

But I didn't notice her problems in our early years together. It seemed to me that all three of us had a lot of fun back then. Once, when we stopped to use an outdoor toilet at a roadside stop, my mother, who was an adept whistler, made the bobwhite call. "If you whistle like this," she said, "the bobwhite bird will answer you." I gave it a try and was delighted to hear an answering call from nearby. Later, I learned that Dad had answered my whistle from the men's outhouse, next door. I don't recall a single incident in later years when my parents were that playful together, but those early years were, apparently, happier times in their marriage.

It was the middle of World War II, and the only tires available were retreads, so a good portion of our time was spent parked beside the road while Daddy changed a flat. Sometimes, though, we rode the train. In those days, the clergy received free passes from most trains, and the one we rode was the Missouri-Kansas-Texas line, also known as the MKT, or "Katy." I loved everything about trains—the hypnotic clatter and sway of the cars as they rolled over the rails, the racket and swoosh of the doors as we moved from car to car, the elegant dining cars with their starched white tablecloths and white-coated waiters, the friendly black porters, the white conductors in their billed caps, and the other passengers—strangers with whom I would start a conversation with the slightest encouragement. "Don't pay any attention to her; she talks too much," Dad would warn them with a smile. I always was a talker.

One of my favorite parts of riding the train was going to Union Station in St. Louis, one of the grandest in the whole USA with its stone castle-like construction and soaring tower. I still remember the majestic sound of rushing water made by the dramatic "Meeting of the Waters" fountain across Market Street from the entrance. St. Louis was among the top 10 cities in the country back then, and Union Station was buzzing with hundreds of travelers. The Fred Harvey Restaurant, the lively snap and bustle of the rags used by the shoeshine "boys" (most of whom were middle-aged black men), and the stands selling newspapers, candy and tobacco all added to the excitement for me.

Many of the travelers were soldiers and sailors on their way to bases in "San Antone'" or elsewhere across the country. Once, while we waited for our train, I watched in fascination as a very young sailor in white cap and bellbottoms alternately cuddled and kissed two heavily made-up young women for what seemed like an hour. Even at such a tender age, I sensed something was wrong with that picture and couldn't take my eyes off them.

The "revivals" Mom and Dad held in small towns and larger cities usually lasted for two weeks and consisted of nightly services Monday through Friday, plus Sunday morning and evening. Saturday was our only night off. Daddy had to come up with a different sermon for every service, but like a campaigning politician, he could recycle his material for a new locale. The Assemblies of God was pretty much a fire-and-brimstone church in those days, and one of Dad's sermons, based on an event in the news, fell into the genre. He told about a tragedy in Texas, in which a little boy had fallen into an oil well hole. Workers had toiled for hours trying to rescue him, but their attempts were in vain. I can still remember the anguish in his voice and see the tears in his eyes as he recounted how the little boy had cried: "Daddy, get me out of here!" As sinners, we are all like that little boy, he explained, but, unlike the men in the story, God's son died to save us from our desperate plight.

Another story, taken from Dad's youth, had a happier ending. While still a teenager, he and some of his cousins and siblings had gone fishing along a riverbank in late afternoon when a dense fog fell just after sundown. As they fumbled around in the darkness, afraid of losing their way or falling into the water, they suddenly saw a light in the distance, shining through the curtain of fog. Someone had made it back to the pick-up truck and turned on the headlights. The analogy to God's love, shining through this dark old world of sin and woe, was obvious. Having heard all the sermons many times, I sometimes spoiled the suspense for those sitting near me by whispering to them about what was coming next.

In the 1940s and '50s, when I was growing up, Assemblies of God people lived in a very closed society because so many "worldly" pleasures like dancing, drinking, smoking, gambling, card-playing, wearing make-up or earrings and going to movies were all forbidden. Outsiders called us "Holy Rollers," because the emphasis was on a personal and often highly emotional contact with God, and a lot of people in the movement took the biblical injunction to "make a joyful noise unto the Lord" very literally, jumping around, shouting and waving their arms in ecstasy, or even, sometimes, rolling on the floor when "moved by the spirit." I'm not sure I ever saw anyone do that, and I sensed that my mother was embarrassed by such public demonstrations of emotion. I know she was a little defensive about the names others had applied to her religion, but she was loyal to it, nevertheless. A bedrock of the movement was its belief in being "filled with the Holy Spirit" and "speaking in tongues," as Jesus' followers were said to do on the Day of Pentecost:

And when the day of Pentecost was fully come, they were all with one accord in one place. And suddenly there came a sound from heaven as of a rushing mighty wind, and it filled all the house where they were sitting. And there appeared unto them cloven tongues like as of fire, and it sat upon each of them. And they were all filled with the Holy Spirit, and began to speak with other languages, as the Spirit gave them utterance. And there were dwelling at Jerusalem Jews, devout men, out of every nation under heaven. Now when this was noised abroad, the multitude came together, and were confounded, because that every man heard them speak in his own language.

Acts II:1-6

Often at the end of a prayer or an enthusiastic chorus during the service, one person might burst into a fit of babble that sound something like this to me: "Heekie ma sheekie ma shundiai. . ." Sometimes a person could go on this way for several minutes while the rest of the congregation sat in silence, convinced that they were getting a direct message from God. When the person finally stopped speaking in tongues, there would be a long, hushed pause while everyone "waited on the Lord" for a translation. And in a few minutes—not always, but often—the same person, or another person, would begin to speak in English, translating the message: "Oh, my people, know that I am God, that I am always with you, that my ways are not your ways, that I can move the highest mountain or part the waves of the greatest sea . . ." the translator might say, or some such thing. When the translator had finished—and it was amazing how long some of them could go on—most of the congregation would raise their arms and praise God together, many with tear-stained faces.

The main emphasis, of course, was a belief in salvation—that, no matter how vile a sinner one might have been, Christ's death on the cross was sufficient to wash away all sins. All one had to do to be "saved" was to believe that Jesus had died for his or her sins. The "infilling of the Holy Spirit," as evidenced by speaking in tongues, would come later, if one earnestly sought it and continued to follow God's path. There is no question in my mind that some people's lives really *were* changed for the better as a result of their finding salvation—I saw it happen in several cases—just as one often sees "hopeless" alcoholics find sobriety through AA. It doesn't pay to underestimate the power of belief or a loving, accepting, like-minded group of fellow human beings.

Strangely enough, though, I don't remember ever seeing either of my parents shouting or speaking in tongues. I have an audiotape of one of my mother's sermons in which she describes her experience of being filled with the Holy Spirit (or Holy Ghost, as it was often called) when she was alone, praying, but I never heard any evidence of it. As for Dad, he dutifully raised his voice from time to time during a sermon to say "Praise the Lord!" or "Hallelujah" or one of the other exclamations commonly heard from the congregation, but neither one of them was the shouting type.

Although Mom was also a licensed and ordained minister with the Assemblies of God, she seldom preached at these meetings. Dad was the preacher and Mom was the piano player and singer. Mom often said that she thought Dad had married her because her ability to play and sing was an asset to an evangelist. Sometimes they would stand me in my little white cowgirl boots up on the altar, where I would sing a popular children's chorus of the day: "I'm in the King's army; I'm in the King's army. I may never march in the infantry, ride in the cavalry, shoot the artillery; I may never fly over Germany, but I'm in the King's army." When I was four years old, I even sang on the radio for one of the churches where we held a meeting.

If the church was large enough to have a radio program, Dad would preach and Mom would sing and play on air. It wasn't too expensive to buy time on small, local stations, so several of the larger churches hosted programs. Mom said once when she was singing and playing, a big fly flew right in her mouth. She couldn't wave it away because she was playing, so she exhaled hard on a word and blew it out without missing a note. She said Dad and the local minister were off to the side in the soundproof studio holding each other up in silent laughter as the fly buzzed around her mouth.

Most of my memories of that time are very happy, but a couple of them stand out, in retrospect, like hints of things to come. Once, when my parents had a fight, Mom threw the alarm clock at Dad. I don't recall the reason for the fight, but I do remember telling people about it, much to my parents' embarrassment. Another time, I apparently did something to make my mother angry and, reaching out to slap me, she slipped and fell on the ice, breaking her watch. I remember the secret pleasure I felt that she had suffered in trying to hurt me.

One summer when I was about 4 years old, Mom was determined to realize one of her dreams: to have a permanent home for our family. While Dad was traveling alone, she and I returned to stay with her parents in Illinois. Her dad, my Grandpa Rainbolt, was the foreman for Keeley Brothers Contracting Company in East St. Louis, and he had begun, early, to teach all five of his boys the fundamentals of carpentry. Exempt from those lessons, Mother was nevertheless a quick learner and convinced that she could do whatever was needed, and she was determined to have a house. But first she had to come up with the money, and money was tight in those days.

Our income for many years consisted of whatever came in the offering plate, and since most AG (Assemblies of God) members in those post-Depression years were poor working people, sometimes the pickings were slim. Moreover, the way Mom told it, Dad never let her know exactly how much he had received. He just doled out money to her in small amounts and she had to figure out how to make it last. So when she came up with the idea of building a home for us, she had only $10 to her name—not enough, even back then—to get a construction loan. Mom had two weapons in her arsenal: her family's reputation and a woman's tears.

When Grandma Rainbolt took Mom to see Mr. Lochmann at the Collinsville Building and Loan Association, they knew they were facing daunting odds, and their fears were confirmed when he told them, sadly, that he could not in good conscience authorize a loan for someone with only a $10 down payment. That's when Mom started to cry. We'll never know, of course, if her crying was calculated, but I don't think so; Mom was much more likely to be combative than to use feminine wiles when confronted with obstacles. I think she was just tired and discouraged, having spent the past few years without a home to call her own. In any case, Mr. Lochmann relented. "Well," he said, "your dad is a good customer of ours. If he'll guarantee the loan, we can give you enough to get started."

In later years, Mom often laughed about her inexperience when she and her 17-year-old brother Robert began construction on the house. Uncle Jim, just 22 years old himself, had given Mom a spade and told her to dig a trench for the footings, so many inches deep and so many wide. When he came back later, he loudly declared her work to be the neatest foundation trench he had ever seen in his whole life: She had followed his instructions to the letter, measuring the hole with a ruler and carefully squaring off the edges and corners.

The little three-room house Mom and her brothers built that summer was destined to grow over the next few years to an eight-room, two-story house with two bathrooms, breezeway, basement and attached garage, but for that first year it was just a small box with no basement, a coal stove in the living room and an icebox in the kitchen. The bathroom fixtures were ones Grandpa Rainbolt had salvaged from buildings Keeley Brothers Contracting Company had torn down. We came back to the house from time to time when we weren't on the road, but we didn't live in it continuously until the fall of 1946, because after another year or so of our vagabond existence, Mom and I returned to Texas to begin the best two years of my childhood.

In the summer of 1944, my parents decided that at least one of them would have to settle down so I could go to school. They also needed to keep on making as much money as possible to pay for the house in Collinsville. I never knew just how Mom did it, but she found a job as a piano teacher at the new Southwestern Bible Institute (SBI) in Waxahachie, Texas, and the two of us went to live there while Dad continued to travel as an evangelist.

Although I'm not sure Mom had ever received any formal piano lessons beyond those her mother had given her, she was an accomplished pianist, at least in terms of what was required for Assemblies of God musicians. Not only could she read music, but she could play any song by ear—and in any key. From her mother she had also learned the "do, re, mi" system, so that all she needed to begin playing a song in a specific key was to locate "do." I still have letters she exchanged with her youngest sister, Bess (later called Carolyn) in which the two of them shared the latest Christian choruses by writing out the syllables on a scrap of paper, along with an occasional note about a "diminished" or "augmented" chord. Mom's style, like that of many AG pianists in those days, was heavily influenced by jazz "stride" playing—in which the left hand maintains a steady rhythm with a single bass note on the first and third beats and a chord on the second and fourth, while the right hand plays the melody. Mom was also an excellent accompanist, since she could adjust the key and phrasing to fit all but the most eccentric of singers. She was just what SBI was looking for.

Unlike seminaries in more established denominations, the Assemblies of God Bible schools were literally that—schools where students of both sexes could study the Bible and also get an accredited education. The levels and types of education varied among schools, but Bible study was always central. What is now Southwestern Assemblies of God University was a brand-new institution, Southwestern Bible Institute, that had just moved to the Waxahachie campus a year before Mom and I arrived there in the fall of 1944. It offered classes not only for students in the first two years of college, but also for those in the last two years of high school.

The war was still going on, and housing was in short supply, so landlords could afford to be choosy, even in small Texas towns. I remember being told to stay in the car and keep a low profile while my mother negotiated with prospective landlords, since mothers living alone with small children were not regarded as the best prospective tenants, and equal housing opportunity was a long way from becoming the law of the land. Mom succeeded in procuring an apartment for us upstairs in a large white Victorian house approximately midway between the campus and my elementary school, the name of which I have long since forgotten, but I still remember the names of my first and second-grade teachers (Miss Anna Lee and Miss Lucy) and my principal (Miss Eva), as well as the names and faces of many of my classmates. I have always found it strange, however, that I recall virtually nothing of my life with Mother in that apartment.

But I do remember walking barefoot through puddles on my way from school to the campus on Sycamore Street, where I would run past the empty fish pond on the front lawn and up the stairs of the administration building to my mother's room on the top floor, which contained not only a piano, but a couch on which I could lie and watch her give her students private lessons. I remember being fascinated by one young man whose hands were so large that he could easily span 10 notes, whereas an octave was all most pianists could manage. In the years to come, my relationship with my mother would become extremely rocky, but I always enjoyed listening to her sing and play. If I got bored with listening to the students, though,

I could roam the hall outside, which was lined with tiny practice rooms, each big enough to hold only a piano and bench. The doors to the rooms had glass windows, so you could see if they were occupied, and some of the sound leaked out into the hall, producing a mild cacophony when the rooms were full. There was usually an empty one, though, so I could go in and practice the little songs I had taught myself to play by ear.

Like Union Station in St. Louis, only smaller, the administration building was a gray, stone castle-like structure. Erected in 1902 by Presbyterian Trinity College, it had a special appeal to the vivid imagination of a child raised on stories, as I had been. I loved to climb the steep, winding stairs in the tower to the very top, where I could look out over the whole town from the open spaces in the crenelated walls, and I frequently ran down to the little bookstore in the basement to spend my weekly allowance of 50 cents on candy or soft drinks. Unlike many modern campuses, the buildings at SBI didn't match architecturally. The girls' dorm was a two-and-a-half-story brick building with a wide stone staircase leading up to the front porch (I was entranced by a tiny frog that I caught leaping up those stairs one day), while the less attractive boys' dorm had a peaked roof and a front entrance at ground level. And then there was the gymnasium, of course, where we went to basketball games on Saturday night and graduation in the spring. I have a very vague, dim memory of a large shed where we went, along with a lot of other people from the campus, to wash our clothes on Mondays. It contained perhaps 20 or more wringer washing machines, the water from which ran out to drains in the concrete floor.

Readers unfamiliar with SBI may recognize the name Waxahachie from a different context. It was the location for three Academy Award-winning movies, including "Places in the Heart," starring Sally Fields. The Wikipedia entry for "Tender Mercies" describes the town as "rural Texas," and it was, indeed, still a small town in 1944, but a fairly bustling one just 30 miles from Dallas and 40 miles from Ft. Worth, so it offered plenty of opportunities, even in those days, for the SBI faculty and staff to enjoy the cultural and educational amenities of the big city, and Mom and her friends took advantage of them.

Every Saturday during my first grade year, Mom and some of her SBI colleagues carpooled to Ft. Worth to take courses at the Methodist institution, Texas Wesleyan University. I believe one member of that group was Klaude Kendrick, who was then director of missions for SBI, and who later became the president of Texas Christian University. He and Mother remained friends for the rest of their lives. Because these weekend trips to Ft. Worth started out very early on Saturday morning, I usually stayed overnight on Friday at the home of Mom's boss, Harold Miles, director of the music department. Harold's daughters and I made several crawdad-fishing trips to a nearby creek while our parents were off getting educated. Using raw bacon as bait, we would hold these lobster-like creatures, some of whom were bigger than our hands, gingerly on the sides, away from their scary-looking pincers, and place them in Mason jars to take home to Mrs. Miles. I was told she cooked them for the family, although I never tasted them, and could not have been persuaded to do so after having seen the ugly things alive, but that didn't take anything away from the pleasure of fishing for them.

Before her marriage—and before she started traveling as a musician with a lady evangelist, Mom had obtained some credits toward her bachelor's degree at Illinois Normal, in Bloomington, and she was determined to finish. The commutes from Waxahachie to Texas Wesleyan in Ft. Worth with her colleagues must have provided a welcome break in her normal routine as piano teacher and mother. Always independent, Mom had been pastor of her own church in Paducah, Kentucky, when she met my dad, who came to hold a revival for her. Being the mother of a preschooler while serving as Dad's sidekick during their years on the road might have cramped her style just a bit, but having an income and apartment of her own in Waxahachie—along with the freedom to schedule her own leisure-time activities without consulting Dad—seemed to agree with her.

Even though the Assemblies of God people shunned many "worldly" pleasures, they found ways to entertain themselves. Music was the center of their lives, next only to God, and the singing and playing at morning chapel meetings and evening services had a lively swing. In fact, some of the most famous stars of early rock 'n roll first discovered their musical talents performing for Assemblies of God congregations. During his childhood, Elvis Presley attended AG churches in Tupelo, Mississippi, and Memphis, Tennessee, with his parents, and he allegedly attended all-night gospel quartet concerts at the First Assembly of God and Ellis Auditorium in Memphis in the early 1950s, before his fame took off and he became a symbol of all that was corrupting modern youth. Another famous rock 'n roll star, Jerry Lee Lewis, was expelled from Southwestern Bible Institute after attending for only three months. (An interesting side note is that Lewis's cousin, the televangelist Jimmy Swaggart, was kicked out of the Assemblies of God later on for cavorting with a prostitute.) I'm not sure what Lewis's infraction was, but it could have been any of a whole raft of sins, from holding hands with a girl to drinking or smoking. But those things happened after our time in Waxahachie. I mention them only to give a hint of the free-wheeling rhythm and emotion of the music in which everyone who could carry a tune or play an instrument was invited to participate. Somewhere in the 1960s, Assemblies of God music began to morph into a more hypnotic, New Age-y style, but back then, it had a definite swing, and we all got a great deal of pleasure out of it.

Although she was not a classical pianist, Mom enjoyed classical music as well. Symphony concerts were apparently one of the few public entertainments that were not off limits in those early years of the movement, because I remember traveling to Ft. Worth with Mom and her friends that first year to hear the great blind pianist and entertainer Alec Templeton perform. A highlight of the concert was when people in the audience called out a series of notes at random, from which Templeton composed a musical piece on the spot.

There were also frequent parties among the SBI faculty and staff. One of those parties, hosted by "Monty" and "Mayfield" Montgomery, stands out in my memory. Mayfield, a home economics teacher at SBI, served all kinds of waffles, including chocolate and pecan. That was only one of our many fun activities that year.

The autographs in Mom's SBI yearbook from our first year in Waxahachie suggest that she had many friends and admirers. Her "sweet smile" and "sweet personality"—two things the members of her own family were not inclined to remember her for in later years—were often mentioned in the handwritten notes from her colleagues, and I know that, for many years afterward, she talked about returning to the Ft. Worth area to retire, a dream she never realized.

There was one sad note during that year: On a lovely spring day, shortly before Mom and I were to leave for our home in Collinsville, I saw the flag at half-staff as I walked across the campus. When I got to my mother's room, she told me that President Roosevelt had died, and soon the whole country went into mourning.

I didn't see much of Dad during my first grade year, so it was especially exciting to find him waiting for me on the last day of school. I still remember my delighted giggles when he suggested, as we walked home, that we tell Mama I had failed first grade. What a joke that would be on her!

It didn't dawn on me that she would know we were teasing, since my report card clearly showed "S" for "satisfactory" in every subject all year, except for one "U" in conduct. That one bad grade was the result of two faults that plagued me throughout childhood: the extreme humiliation I felt whenever I made a mistake, and my inability to apologize when a mistake hurt others. I have long since learned to apologize when I am wrong or offend someone, but I still cringe when I make a mistake, and back then, I was unable to humble myself sufficiently to apologize. On the occasion that resulted in the bad mark on my report card, I had unwittingly walked between Miss Anna Lee and one of the parents while they were talking. When she grabbed my shoulder and pulled me back, ordering me to say "excuse me," I was too mortified—and too stubborn—to comply. So I spent the rest of the day in the principal's office, and my otherwise unblemished report card had that one memorable stain.

The punishment wasn't all bad, though. I was secretly in love with Miss Eva, the principal, who had snow-white, carefully coiffed hair, long, lacquered nails, and a predilection for bright purple dresses. Making me sit all day in her office listening to the tap of her nails on the typewriter keys and the jangle of her multiple bangle bracelets was rather like throwing Bre'r Rabbit into the briar patch.

So I'm sure my mother knew I hadn't failed first grade, but what Daddy proposed was a delightful joke for a primary schooler. To top it off, he brought great news: He was going to be joining us at SBI the following fall as dean of men, and we would be living in the boys' dormitory!

In 1945, we learned that World War II had finally ended. I was only six years old, and since the war ended in stages, I'm not sure whether we were in Collinsville or Waxahachie at the time, but I have a mental image of happily hanging out the window of our car, ringing a cowbell while Dad drove Mom and me through streets of people shouting and honking their horns.

When we arrived back in Waxahachie that fall, we moved into an apartment on the first floor of the boys' dormitory. If Mom ever cooked during my second-grade year, I don't remember it. We did have a kitchen in our little apartment, but I don't think we spent much time in it. Most of the time, we took our meals in the cafeteria in the basement of the girls' dormitory. Standing in line waiting our turn, we would join the students in singing gospel choruses and funny ditties. On days when I failed to get up in time to make it to the cafeteria, Dad would take me to the little diner across the street for breakfast. Mom would already be at work, teaching piano, but Dad's duties as dean of men were more flexible, so we got to spend some precious time together. A daddy's girl, I was never happier than when I had his full attention.

Life was safer for children back then, so I was pretty free to wander around the campus and nearby places in the neighborhood on my own, even though I was only seven. Sometimes I would go across the street to the soda fountain and order a Dr. Pepper and a bag of peanuts. I loved to pour the peanuts into my soda bottle and eat them as I drank my Dr. Pepper, as I had seen some other people do. On other days, I would visit my best friend from school, Mary Neal Daniel, at her house a couple of blocks away and spend some time sitting up in the apple tree in her back yard with her and her little brother, Danny. On special evenings, Mom, Dad and I—usually in the company of several friends from the college faculty or administration—would go into town for burgers at the Red Rose Café, a friendly hangout for faculty and students.

While Mom's routine was in many ways the same as it had been the year before, she had some added duties in that second year. She and Dad sometimes worked as a team to corral the high spirits of their young charges in the boys' dormitory, many of whom were still in high school. On occasion, the boys' rowdy play would disturb the more serious students and Dad would have to calm them down. But since the building was three stories high, the boys had developed a warning system that enabled them to keep one step ahead of him. So Dad devised a trick of his own. On especially chaotic nights, he would have Mom throw the main switch at the fuse box downstairs, plunging the whole building into darkness. Mom would then count to thirty, by which time Dad had sprinted up the stairs, two at a time, to the top floor. When Mom turned the lights back on, the boys would be caught in the act. I suspect this game was a lot more fun for them than for Dad. Fortunately, though, he was in his early thirties and in great shape. Occasionally, he punished the worst offenders by having them do chores. I'll never forget seeing one of them, an especially rascally boy with blond hair, mopping the dorm floor in his nightshirt. Dad also frequently had boys chase golf balls for him when he practiced his putting and drives. That year, my parents had started playing golf together. I have vague memories of walking along a course with the two of them, but my memories are clearer of Dad hoisting a bag of clubs to go out for a game with his buddies later on, when he and Mom had stopped playing together.

During that second year in Waxahachie, Mom and Dad were still partners in many ways. Dad was pastor of the new college church, which aired a weekly radio show, for which Dad preached and Mom played, sang and directed some of the musical groups. Their live radio program aired on Saturday mornings, when she would have been traveling to classes in Ft.

Worth with her colleagues, so she had to postpone finishing her degree. Although I remember that year as one of the best of my life, it's possible that Mom might have preferred the one before, when she had enjoyed more independence. Still, it must have been a relative heaven for her. She didn't have to cook or do much cleaning, she had a paying job that offered her a place in the spotlight (something she always enjoyed), and she and Dad were making enough money together to pay off our little house in Illinois at a rapid pace. Her childcare duties were also significantly reduced because the whole student body had become my baby-sitters.

Part of the reason I was so popular with the students was my skill as a secret courier for love notes between the girls and their boyfriends. The rules were strict back then—so strict that Dad tried, with little effect, to get the administration to loosen up a little. Couples could not even hold hands, and they were reprimanded if they spent too much time standing alone talking to each other. Dates for the older students had to be chaperoned, so one of the only ways for young lovers to communicate privately was through the notes they entrusted to me. I guess I proved to be a reliable courier, because the girls often let me spend the night with them in the dormitory. We had a lot of fun on those nights—like the time we sneaked down to the cafeteria to steal condiments and syrup off the tables to put on our Ritz crackers. The boys liked me, too, and several of them promised to wait for me to grow up. Almost a decade later, I got a rude shock when Thurman Thomas, a trombonist who had promised to wait for me, came to the church my parents were pastoring to hold a revival. To my dismay, he brought a wife and baby with him!

While private dates were forbidden at SBI, co-ed activities were another matter. Songfests, club meetings, banquets and basketball games in the gym on Saturday nights were some of the highlights of campus life. The girls would attend those Saturday night games with their hair in pin curls wrapped in bandanas, Rosie the Riveter style, since nothing could be allowed to interfere with their Sunday morning curly hairdos. My own Shirley Temple curls were produced with the aid of metal curlers Mom put in my hair on nights before special occasions. I apparently didn't mind sleeping on them, but they were a definite irritant to me in another way: "How did you get such pretty curls?" the big girls would ask me, to which I would reply, "My mother puts up my hair on tin curlers," to which they would respond, feigning misunderstanding, "Ten curlers? What kind of curlers? We didn't ask you how many." Their good-natured teasing always frustrated and embarrassed me. I never liked to be laughed at, even if the laughter was kindly.

It probably sounds comical now to say that one of my favorite activities that year on the SBI campus was slopping the hogs. In those low-tech days, the college maintained a small farm that existed in a symbiotic relationship with the school. I don't know whether the pigs were slaughtered for cafeteria meals, but I do know that every day before sundown, one of the students named Johnny would load up a wooden sled with a large barrel of garbage from the cafeteria and take it out to the feed the pigs. The sled was pulled by two mules, which I named "Brownie" and "Midnight," and I delighted in riding along on these trips. If it smelled awful, which it surely did, I didn't notice. And if I got in Johnny's way, he never complained. He always seemed glad to have me along.

Overall, those first few years of my life were a virtual paradise. Things were about to change drastically, however.

In the summer of 1946, when we returned to the house in Collinsville, neighbors told us that during the winter lightning had struck a power pole, causing a ball of fire to roll along the lines to our house. Luckily, no serious damage was done, but, in retrospect, I think the fireball was a fitting symbol for what our lives would be like in that house for the next few years.

We didn't return to Waxahachie that fall. I never knew all the reasons. Publicly, Dad said that chasing after the boys was just too physically exhausting for him. Privately, he told me later that Mom had managed to get crossways with some of the people there and made life difficult for him—a scenario that seemed plausible in light of some of her behavior later on. But, looking back at all those kind notes in Mom's yearbook from her first year at SBI—all the students and colleagues who commented on her "sweet smile" and kind and caring personality—I wonder if there could be another side to the story.

The fact that Mom's yearbook from the second year contained no comments from her colleagues would seem to support Dad's version of why we didn't return to SBI, but some time shortly after our return to Illinois, I found a letter in the kitchen, signed by someone named "Violet" and addressed to Dad, that read disturbingly like a love letter. I don't remember any specific sentences—just that reading the letter made me feel uncomfortable, and I was afraid to tell anyone about it. Many years later, when I asked Dad about it, he claimed to have no memory of the letter or anyone named Violet, but while I was going through the old yearbooks from SBI in the process of writing this book, I found a photo of a student named Violet. After our move to Illinois, my mother frequently accused my dad of having affairs, so, in retrospect, I can't help wondering if the Violet from SBI was the one whose letter had disturbed me so.

The summer started out pleasantly enough, though. Dad went back on the road alone for a while, and during his absence, Mom decided to surprise him by having her brothers construct a garage near one side of the house. When Dad returned home, he decided to connect the garage to the house with a "breezeway" porch. I still remember some of our neighbors helping him to tamp down the concrete with 2x4's. Later, while Uncle Bob was working to screen in the breezeway, he overheard me telling Barbara, a neighbor girl, that Johnny Matikitis was going to marry me when he grew up because I was "more beautifuller" than she was. I was embarrassed when he laughingly told my mother about it.

Although I hadn't yet started taking piano lessons, I had picked up a lot from watching my mother play, and I was already able to play some simple songs by ear. I remember "teaching" the neighborhood children to play the piano by showing them the "beginning" and "ending" chords and the "in-between" chords that I had learned from watching Mom. Apparently, I started assuming the role of a more mature, knowledgeable person than my peers very early in life.

While Dad was away that summer, Mom was filling in for a local pastor, Sister Hisserick, who was having some health problems, and perhaps that's how she got the money to build the garage. I don't know how Mom got the job as substitute minister, but Sister Hisserick died soon thereafter, and in the fall of 1946, Mom and Dad became co-pastors of Bethel Tabernacle Assembly of God Church at 89th and State Streets in East St. Louis, Illinois, just seven miles from our home in Collinsville via Illinois Route 157.

Two decades later, when East St. Louis became a major hot spot in the growing Black Power movement, industries and better-off residents, mostly white, began moving away, and the city went into a tailspin from which it never recovered. But when Mom and Dad took the church just after World War II, business was booming. Monsanto, the railroads, stockyards, meatpacking houses and other industries in the area were all thriving. The town had always been largely blue-collar, though, and blacks and whites had often found themselves in competition for jobs. According to Mom, her dad was a witness to the 1917 race riot—one of the worst in U.S. history—that was sparked when the Aluminum Ore company brought in 470 African-American workers to replace white workers who had gone on strike. During that riot, he told her, whites had set fire to the homes of African-Americans and shot at the people who lived in them when they tried to escape. I would like to think that Grandpa didn't take part in this carnage, but Mom did tell me he had belonged to the Klan at one time. He told her it was not a racist organization when he belonged to it, but one to protect the unions against management. After I was grown, Mom gave me a book called *Bloody Williamson: A Chapter in American Lawlessness*, by Paul M. Angle, which described some of the violence in Southern Illinois' Williamson County, but after seeing a couple of photos of lynchings in it, I was so upset that I put it down without reading it.

Several members of our little church had migrated north from Arkansas, and their views on race reflected those of the South. In contrast, although Dad had been born in Texas, he was as color-blind as any person I have ever known, and he had begun early sharing his views on racial equality with me, giving me books to read about how blacks had suffered during slavery and the still-extant Jim Crow laws. These books and Dad's frequent comments that blacks were "just people" like everyone else, inspired in me a lifelong sympathy for their struggle. I have a vague memory, in fact, of attending, with my parents, at least one black revival meeting in my early childhood, standing on the periphery outside the tent, and I was told that my dad's parents had been married by a black minister, which would have been extremely rare in their times. In the beginning of the Pentecostal movement, both women and African-Americans had played a significant role, and today many Assemblies of God congregations are well integrated, but I didn't see any African-Americans in the churches we visited during my childhood or youth, and none ever ventured to attend our services at the church in East St. Louis. So, in my teens, I often found myself at odds with both adults and young people in our congregation over the issue of race. At least once during my teens, one of them accused me of being a "nigger lover."

In the beginning, though, I was happy with life in our new church. Although not the center of attention I had been on the road or on the SBI campus, I still enjoyed a certain status as the preacher's daughter that I had come to take for granted, and being an outgoing child, I got along well with both children and adults. I especially liked the old people. They always seemed to me like young people trapped in old bodies.

Even though Mom no longer had a separate income and set of friends like those she had enjoyed in Waxahachie, she didn't seem unhappy during those first months in Collinsville, either. But everything changed when, at almost 36, she discovered that she was pregnant. From some of the things she told me later, I think she had not been very careful about birth control after I was born. She said she had prayed for a baby for four years before I came along (which, in keeping with her tendency to dramatize things, was a bit of an exaggeration, since I was born less than four years after her marriage), so maybe she thought she couldn't get pregnant again. In any event, her pregnancy with my little brother was obviously a big surprise. Mom had spent a good part of her growing up years caring for her younger siblings, and from her stories of those years, I got the impression that she had pretty much had her fill of child care long before she was married.

That's not to say that she was a bad mother to me in my early years. In addition to teaching me a lot of things before I even entered school, she had breastfed me for nine months. She liked to tell the story about how people along the route from Highlands, Texas, to Collinsville, Illinois, had been amazed to find a woman driving with only a nursing baby for company when she took me to visit her parents during the first few months of my life. (She would confess many years later that she had originally planned to leave my dad on that trip, but my guess is that her parents told her to go back to her husband and do her duty. Grandma Rainbolt, who had eight children in 22 years, still had a preschooler at home to care for when I was born.) Until our move to Illinois, though, Mom had seldom experienced the traditional life of a housewife and mother. She had always received considerable help with childcare from members of our congregation, and in Waxahachie, the students often took me off her hands. So not only had Mom been relieved of some of the traditional burdens of motherhood for much of my early childhood; she had held down jobs that made good use of her talents and kept her in the spotlight. But everything had already begun to change after our move to Illinois.

For one thing, we lived out on the semi-rural edge of a small town, miles from most of the members of our congregation and light years away from the exciting bustle of the campus we had left behind. For another, we had only one car, in which Dad was gone for a good part of many days, visiting the sick, calling on church members, or combing through second-hand bookstores or private collections, looking for rare books. So Mom didn't get away from the house or have much company, except for family members, several of whom, including her parents, lived in our town. Uncle Jim and Aunt Elsie actually lived next door to us, just across the empty lot that soon became Dad's large and bountiful vegetable garden. I know Mom enjoyed being so close to her family—they were extremely tight—but she must have longed, sometimes, for the days when she had run around with her friends in Waxahachie, taking trips to Dallas and Ft. Worth and attending parties and other social events.

Another drawback was that our income was almost certainly lower than it had been at SBI. Mom and Dad had both held down salaried jobs at the school, whereas now they were co-pastors of a tiny church, dependent on what came in the offering plate on Sunday. Worse still, once Dad joined her as co-pastor, people immediately reacted to him as the pastor and to Mom as the pastor's wife. Dad's good looks, caring personality and unpretentious style encouraged people to let their hair down in his presence, and Mom had a hard time competing with that. Virtually everyone seemed to enjoy her singing and playing, and on the few occasions when she gave the sermon, they seemed to like that, too. Listening to her it was more like hearing a story with a moral than the listening to the kinds of sermons people were used to hearing in Assemblies of God churches. She could help her listeners see the characters of the Bible as real people, with brothers and sisters, parents and children, problems and challenges just like their own. But she tended to have a sterner mien and less sociable personality than Dad. And even though the Assemblies of God was way out front of the times in recognizing women as ministers, plain old-fashioned male chauvinism still helped to "keep her in her place." Mom's nature had never been that of a subordinate, so all these things, along with being unexpectedly pregnant at almost 36, and then having to care for a new baby, were bound to seriously cramp her style.

At first, I was very excited about having a little brother, and throughout his childhood I took as much pride in him as if he had been my own baby. I had been born at home, in Highlands, Texas, but by the time John came along, women in the city were spending a week or more in the hospital after giving birth, so Dad and I had those days at home alone together. That may be when I discovered that he was a pretty good cook. Fried potatoes with the skins on and "bulldog" gravy—basically white sauce dotted with pepper—were two of his specialties. When Dad went to Christian Welfare Hospital in East St. Louis to visit Mom and his new son, I rode along, but children weren't allowed to visit in those days, so Dad stood me on top of our car to let me wave at Mom as she smiled at me out the window. And when she finally brought John home on a very hot day in July of 1947, my first memory is of leaning over his bassinet to breathe in the wonderful smell of baby powder and lotion. The temperatures were stifling, so John's bassinet was out on the breezeway to catch as much fresh air as possible, and it was covered with mosquito netting to protect him from bites. I was immediately drawn to this fascinating, cuddly little bundle of flesh that was my brother.

The first signs of trouble were John's nightly colic. Later Mom would say that maybe the smell of new paint in the kitchen had tainted her milk, or that the baby wasn't getting enough to eat from nursing, but my guess is that postpartum depression had transmitted itself to her infant son, who cried loudly and inconsolably for more than an hour every night at six o'clock, our normal supper hour. I think it was during this time that Mom's younger sister Edith, her husband, Jack, and their preschooler son were living temporarily in our garage (which Dad had already converted to a library) while work on their own house was being completed. I have vague memories of even Uncle Jack, who was definitely not the maternal type, trying to help relieve Mom during the baby's crying. But I was the main person to whom that responsibility fell while Mom, who had turned into a vicious crazy person, cleaned up after dinner.

After my brother was grown, when he and Mom had a serious falling out during his college years, I was haunted by guilt feelings about what I had whispered in his ear while I was walking him back and forth on the breezeway, bouncing on the balls of my feet and patting him on the back. "Never love your mother!" I had told him, tears streaming down my cheeks.

After my brother's birth, things grew steadily worse between Mom and me. She turned into a frightening monster who frequently yelled at Dad and me. More than once, she told me I was driving her crazy, and I actually began to wonder if, somehow, I was to blame for her crazy behavior. "Get up off your ass, you lazy hound! I'm the only one who does any work around here," she would shout at me. And once, when John was still a toddler, she was beating me so fiercely that he got scared and started crying.

Even Dad, who had always been so kind, occasionally lost his temper with me. When John fell out of his high chair, Dad came running into the kitchen hollering, "If you ever let him fall out of that high chair again, I'll half kill you!" Another time, after he told me to pick up the pots and pans John had scattered all over the kitchen floor, he yelled at me and pulled my hair when I responded in exasperation, "Clean them up yourself."

So much had changed. Just a few years earlier, I had told myself while lying in bed on the foldout davenport in our little three-room house in Collinsville, "These sheets smell like my mama," and the thought had been warm and comforting. Now there was no comfort to be found anywhere.

It seemed as if Mom and Dad got into loud arguments almost every night. Raised in a household in which her mother had put supper on the table promptly at five o'clock each evening for her carpenter husband, Mom had absorbed the family tradition of rigid routine and the One Right Way to Do Everything. While suppertime in our house was at six to accommodate the different schedule of a preacher's family, she was livid if

Dad did not appear on the dot to join us at the table. Dad, always absent-minded, had been raised in a much more loosey-goosey household, not to mention that he had been on the road for much of his life, so he had trouble adjusting to Mom's new, tight schedule. Too often, he would show up when dinner was getting cold, at which point all hell would break loose, with Mom demanding to know where he had been and loudly accusing him of being with some woman. Perhaps he was—after awhile I thought I wouldn't blame him, since who wouldn't choose some other woman over the harridan that Mom had become? But I suspect that, usually, he had simply lost track of time or wasn't in any hurry to come home to what had become a very unpleasant atmosphere.

Their arguments often continued well into the night, with Mom on the offense and Dad playing defense. If he tried to apologize, Mom would respond with "Sorry! You're sorry? Sorry doesn't help! You shouldn't have done it in the first place!" When he tried to hug or kiss her, she would shrug him off and turn away. When he offered what she called an "excuse" for some transgression, she would reply with one word: "Shit!" Mom had so conditioned me against bad language, not even allowing me to say "golly," or "gee," that to hear her say "shit" was beyond shocking for me. But one night when John was about four years old, I heard her say something far worse. It was after we had added a wing to the house, and I was lying in the dark in my upstairs bedroom, listening as they argued below. "John is all I have in the world," she cried.

Hearing those words made me feel as if I had been thrown overboard. "What about me, Mom?" I thought.

It would be wrong to leave the impression, though, that the years in Collinsville were all bad. We lived on the edge of town, and next to the house across the street was a hilly woods, where Johnny Matikitis and I liked to build "huts" by digging holes in the ground, making a roof with branches and leaves. Once, before my brother was born, Johnny and I, intent on creating a "swimming pool," had dug a shallow hole at the bottom of the hill behind his house. In my mind, it is about five feet wide and maybe a couple of feet deep. I guess Johnny's dad must have given us part of a bag of cement, because we even stirred up enough "concrete" to make one flagstone in a pitiful attempt to line the pool. As luck would have it, that year a major flood hit the area. Mama said she thought God had changed his mind about his promise to Noah because it rained so hard for so many days that much of the East St. Louis bottomland was underwater. On our bluff in Collinsville, though, we were fine, but rain filled up our "swimming pool," and I have vague memories of floating a washtub in it.

Up at the end of the street, the Waggoner's farmhouse overlooked hilly pastureland with cows, sheep, a horse named "Amber," a sheep dog named "Lady," and other animals, including baby ducks with downy coats and darling little orange webbed feet. Once in awhile, I got to ride Amber, and often I spent the better part of the day on the hills, lying on the ground, listening to the cows munch on the grass as a plane buzzed far overhead. In some of the most trying periods of my life, I have often escaped in memory to those peaceful times out on a hillside in the pasture. On hot days, I liked to take a "swim" in the horse trough, and as the day cooled down, I would sometimes join a game of "horse" or "21" with Donny and Jimmy Waggoner and other neighborhood kids around the basketball hoop that hung on the side of the barn. When my parents wanted me to come home, they just honked the car horn, the sound of which carried far out over the hills.

The neighbor ladies, in whose houses I loved to sit and talk while they worked, were kind to me. Mrs. Wendler, who knew I loved cheesecake, would buy me a piece when the driver of the bakery truck, which came honking through our neighborhood, stopped to open up the back of the truck and display his delicious treats. It was the old, dense kind of cheesecake, probably made from ricotta, with a doughy crust—not like the cream cheese or airy gelatin stuff that seems more common today. When Johnny's mother fried up a batch of Lithuanian potato pancakes, she always invited me over for a taste. Made from shredded raw potatoes, eggs, and other mysterious ingredients, they were crispy and delicious—still the best I've ever tasted.

I don't remember Mom ever hugging me or saying, "I love you" during those years, but she *did* things for me, like sewing my clothes, accompanying me in my vocal and instrumental recitals, and teaching me to sing harmony. While Dad was demonstrative, Mom maintained that she showed her love through hard work. From her father she had absorbed the attitude that work was a virtue and Sloth one of the Seven Deadly Sins, so she was a very hard worker. Once, I saw her paint a room and sew pleated, lined draperies for it in the same day. After these herculean exertions, she would often collapse for two or three days with what she called a "sick headache." But as long as she could stand on her feet, she was always working to help me and the whole family.

The best times I remember with Mom from our years in Collinsville, though, were our vacations. While our family took several vacations together, Mom and I also evolved a tradition of women-only trips. Since Dad liked to browse secondhand bookstores when he traveled—an activity the rest of us found tedious—we started striking out on road trips of our own. Accompanied by my Grandmother Rainbolt, we drove up to Detroit and under the tunnel to Windsor, Canada, to visit Grandma's sister. Another time we went down to Galveston, Texas, to visit Aunt Bess. I don't remember where John was during these women-only trips, but I assume he was at home being cared for by Dad. Whenever we traveled, though, whether women-only or with the whole family, Mom seemed in a much better mood than at home, and we usually had a very good time. She was almost like a different person when we were on the road.

But when adults asked me how old I wanted to be, even before John was born, I would say "five" or "six," because those early years still seemed like the best of my life so far. I think I would have adjusted to life in Collinsville eventually, though, had it not been for the trauma of my mother's postpartum depression and our deteriorating relationship.

The next summer, when I was nine years old, I was sent to Texas to stay with a woman who had cared for me when my dad pastored there. When I was between the ages of six months and two-and-a-half years, we had lived in Electra, a little oil town in northwest Texas, about 30 miles from Archer City, where "The Last Picture Show" was later filmed. I had only a vague memory or two from our years there, but a woman in the church had often taken me home with her, and I think Dad must have decided she would be the perfect person for me to spend some time with, considering all our family was going through. "Ray" (actually her last name but the only name I ever called her) was very different from my mother: warm, easygoing, not too much of a stickler for the rules, and very indulgent of her own daughters, who were young adults by the time of my first visit.

In later years, Mom told me with disapproval that Ray used to wash the dishes for her teen-aged girls so they wouldn't ruin their manicures, and, during my visit Ray pampered me as much, or even more, than she had pampered her own daughters. She altered their dresses to fit me and took me swimming at the city pool. A lot of our church members back then didn't approve of mixed bathing, but Ray was more laid back and not averse to breaking a rule that didn't make sense to her. Using a playsuit pattern, she sewed me a yellow terrycloth swimsuit and walked with me every day alongside the dusty cobblestone streets that led to the city swimming pool. On our way, we would pass the home of Sister Cornelius, a pillar of the church who was famous for having been the Sunday School teacher of several boys who grew up to be preachers. "Hello, Sister Cornelius," Ray would call sweetly to the old lady sitting on the front porch as we passed, "We're just going out for a little walk." After we reached the pool, having gone a roundabout way so Sister Cornelius wouldn't suspect anything, Ray would sit outside the fence and watch me paddle around in the shallow end until I was ready to leave.

When Ray put me on the train to go back home that first year before my tenth birthday, there were tears in my eyes.

A couple of summers later when I went back for a visit, Texas was in the midst of a severe drought. The grass, where it had managed to survive at all, was as stiff and yellow as straw, and the pool was closed. Ray's house wasn't air-conditioned—only the rich had air conditioning back then—but she made sure I was comfortable on her bed in front of the window fan, a "swamp cooler" which made a comforting hum and threw out tiny droplets of water. I spent whole afternoons there reading comic books from a big pile in a box she had thoughtfully set beside the bed. When I wanted more entertainment, I wandered around the house, examining the shelves of knick-knacks Ray and Papa Ray had bought at tourist shops along Route 66: cedar boxes, tiny wooden outhouses, corncob pipes. Sometimes I amused myself by playing 78 records of Homer and Jethro singing "I'm My Own Grandpa" or Spike Jones' band playing crazy songs in which bells, whistles, car horns and God only knows what other implements were employed as musical instruments. They never failed to make me laugh.

Ray and I had Coke floats—my favorite—almost every day, and to this day, the sweet sting of a Coke float on my tongue can flood me with memories of Ray's love and those happy vacations with her and her family in Texas. Papa Ray always bought big, juicy, Texas watermelons for me, and Ray made sure I had everything else I loved to eat: white buttermilk cornbread, longhorn cheese, enchiladas, and salmon croquettes, dipped in cornmeal and fried. Once I even had fried chicken for breakfast. And when I tried to help with the dishes, Ray would wave me away. "You'll have plenty of work to do when you get home," she would say. Maybe Dad had told her how things were at home, or else she just surmised from having been our close neighbor during my earliest years that Mom could be a pretty strict taskmaster for a little girl.

Several times a week, we went to church, enjoying the lively singing, and on Sunday afternoons, Ray let me go home with other girls from the church. I made friends with an older girl there named Yvonne who played the xylophone for church services. I still called her "Bonnie," a carryover from when my parents had pastored there and I had been too little to pronounce her name. To my delight, Bonnie let me play around on the xylophone after services.

I would go back to Electra for one more memorable vacation before my 15th birthday. On the last visit, I was already pregnant with Ronnie's baby, although I didn't know it at the time.

To understand the impact of the changes my parents were going through after our move, one would have to know more about their early lives, before they met. They had a number of things in common: Both were eldest children of large families (Mom had five brothers and three sisters, and Dad had four brothers and six sisters). Both had grown up with harsh fathers and more loving mothers. Both had struck out on their own while still in their teens. And, of course, both were Pentecostal ministers by the time they met. But the differences between them were significant, and those differences became more obvious once we left Texas to settle on my mother's home turf in Illinois.

Later in life, when I got to know a number of people who had grown up in alcoholic homes, I saw a striking resemblance between the stories they told and Mom's descriptions of her own childhood. "We learned to talk without moving our lips," Mom told me, recalling how she and her brothers and sisters had communicated when their dad was in a temper. "Watch out—here he comes!" they would whisper, their lips stretched tightly over their teeth and their jaws locked in place. Although Mom's dad wasn't an alcoholic himself, one of his brothers had abandoned a wife and several children for drink, and there is some reason to suspect that my great-grandfather was overly fond of the bottle, too, which may explain why Grandpa was so strict with his children. Although Grandma was a churchgoer and even played the piano for services, Grandpa never attended, but it still seemed as if he was afraid there was a devil in his family that would come out if his children were not tightly controlled.

Mom was born on January 29, 1912, in Creal Springs, a tiny town in the "Little Egypt" area of Southern Illinois, which her maternal grandfather had helped to found. She went to high school in nearby Marion and graduated at sixteen from high school in East St. Louis, where her carpenter father had moved the family to follow construction jobs. The eldest of eight children, Mom said she was given a lot of responsibility for her siblings but virtually no authority, so she often found herself in a no-win situation: Once when her brother Jim was totally out of control while she was caring for him, she tied a clothesline around his waist and fastened it to a tree. Anybody who knew Uncle Jim could testify that he probably would have been classified as ADHD if he had been born a couple of generations later—even Grandpa had trouble handling him—but when Grandpa found out what Mom had done, *she* was the one who got the beating.

Mom told me more than once how her teachers had taken her out into the hall to cluck over the bruises from her father's beatings. Working in construction, Grandpa often had to drive around town, and Mom said she lived in constant terror that he would pass by the schoolyard one day and see her wearing the bloomers that were required for gym class. "If I ever catch you in that outfit, I'll jerk you right out of school and teach you a lesson you won't forget!" he had warned her.

In many ways, Mom's mother was a very strong woman and a definite matriarch, but for reasons that have always seemed inexplicable to me, she was unable to protect Mom from Grandpa's violence. Grandma had several older brothers who could probably have taken Grandpa on, or if necessary, it seemed that she could have gone home to her parents. But maybe she was too proud to ask for help. As the thirteenth and rather spoiled child of relatively prosperous self-made German immigrants in Southern Illinois, she had "married beneath herself" by wedding a carpenter from a less distinguished family. Perhaps she was determined to show that she had made the right choice. Or maybe she just assumed it was the role of fathers to be disciplinarians and mothers not to interfere. I guess a lot of women felt that way in those days. But, according to Mom, Grandma once said to her,

"I don't know how you can love your dad." It always seemed to me like a strange comment for her to make in light of the fact that she and Grandpa seemed to get along pretty well and stayed married until his death, long after all their children were grown.

In going through some papers while writing this book, I was surprised to find a couple of letters Grandpa had written to Mom from Ft. Meyers, Florida, where he and Grandma used to go for winter vacations after his retirement, and I was struck by two things: the almost illiterate quality of his writing, and his comments about how much he missed his children. In contrast to Grandma, who was valedictorian of her high school graduating class, Grandpa had dropped out of school after fifth grade to help support his family. His children all said he was tremendously capable and great at teaching them all kinds of things from how to drive a car to how to build a house, and Mom said he even helped her with her math homework, but he was probably under a lot of strain trying to prove himself to his better-off in-laws by providing for a growing family without the aid of a formal education or their social advantages. He was a wonderful grandpa to me, but I guess he took his frustration out on his eldest child, who was as strong-willed and stubborn as he was. Some things are just hard to figure out.

When Mom was 17, Grandpa kicked her out of the house for an unspecified infraction of the rules. She lived with a couple of aunts for a while, working at various jobs—waitress, nanny for a Jewish family, clerk in a hardware store. That was her "wild" period, in which she smoked cigarettes (something I didn't learn until I was in my thirties) and danced with a bucket of beer on her head (something she liked to tell me in my youth to show how popular she had been, and what a good dancer).

By the time Mom was approaching twenty, she had an offer to go on the road with a dance band as a singer and pianist, but at some point her Pentecostal upbringing caused her to repent of her sins, and she decided, instead, to join the all-female musical retinue of a lady evangelist. For a little while, the whole group settled down to pastor a church in a rented room of a tobacco barn in Paducah, Kentucky, but soon the lady evangelist, who apparently had an itchy foot, decided to hit the road again, taking her musicians with her. The way Mom told it, two of the deacons from the church pursued the group to a neighboring town and begged Mom to come back and pastor the church on her own, so that's how she started preaching.

And that's how she met my dad.

"If you want to know what my family was like growing up," Dad said to me when I was around 12 years old, "just read this book." Handing me a copy of The Grapes of Wrath, he added, "We were Okies." Dad's family didn't migrate to California like the people in Steinbeck's book, but they were poor, uneducated wanderers in Oklahoma and Texas, where Dad was born, in Dripping Springs, on December 16, 1913. His father was an itinerant Pentecostal preacher who must have been one of the very first ones in the Assemblies of God movement, which was just starting to take shape around the time of Dad's birth. Moving from town to town, they always had a cow for milk, Dad said, but often very little else.

Grandpa Chamless might have been religious, but that didn't keep him from beating his children, just as Mom's father did. Dad's younger brother Wes said that once, after Grandpa had given Dad an especially savage beating, Dad had pretended to run away from home but sneaked back while Grandpa was out of the house and hid in the attic for a couple of weeks until the heat was off. He was kept alive by the food his brothers and sisters sneaked up to him with his mother's help, and he entertained himself by reading paperback westerns. "As long as he had something to read, Paul was happy," Uncle Wes said. A few days later, after things cooled down, Dad came down out of the attic, walked down the road a way, then turned around and pretended to be returning home. At one point during his early teens when Grandpa started to beat him, Dad instinctively fought back. He must have got the best of his dad that day, because I don't think he was ever beaten again. But he told me he was always ashamed of himself for having raised his hand to his father.

Standing 6 ft. tall and weighing 175 pounds at the age of 17, Dad was handsome, strong and muscular, a good runner and swimmer. He was embarrassed about his lack of formal education and always avoided saying how far he had gone in school. For years I thought he had completed at least a year or two of high school because he had talked about being a good high jumper in his teens. But I found out the real story from Uncle Wes after Dad's death. Wes said one time Dad read a newspaper story about the Olympic Games and made up his mind to try out for them. He would have been twelve years old in the summer of 1926, which must have been when he decided to train for the Olympics. Enlisting his siblings as timers and record-keepers, he worked at sprinting, long jump, high jump and discus. Uncle Wes said he used a manhole cover for a discus, but more likely it was something lighter from around the farm on which they lived. In any case, it was heavy enough to give Aunt Rachel a hefty scar under her eye when she accidentally got in the way, and Dad was so upset about hurting his little sister that he abandoned his Olympic ambitions then and there. Aunt Rachel carried the scar all her life, but like all of Dad's siblings, she didn't carry a grudge against Dad. They were all crazy about him.

Dad's mother was clearly devoted to him, as well. By the time I knew her, she was a shapeless little lady with a straggly bun on the back of her head, which shook uncontrollably whenever we came to visit her in her big Victorian rooming house in Springfield, Missouri. "Oh, it's my boy! It's Paul! It's my boy!" she would cry in delight, her head wobbling wildly. But the photos of her in the early days of her marriage showed a beautiful woman with a touch of the rebel in her. In a formal portrait from early in their marriage, she and Grandpa are posing with their first two boys, Dad and Ezra, in the traditional style of the time: Grandpa seated, looking dignified and serious with the boys on his lap, and Grandma in her wasp-waisted, high collared dress, standing behind. Only Grandma isn't standing stiff and straight like most women in those old pictures. Instead, she is leaning over on one elbow with a hand on Grandpa's shoulder, head cocked, finger to her cheek and a mischievous gleam in her eye. That playful streak lasted all of her life. Shortly after her death, when her children were sitting around the kitchen table reminiscing about her, one of her children confessed that he had been her favorite child. "That's not true," another responded. "I was Mama's favorite—she told me so!" After more discussion, they all had a big laugh when they discovered that Grandma had told each one, privately, "You're my favorite—but don't tell the others."

As the photos show, Grandma Chamless was a real beauty in her youth. She told me she had an 18-inch waist and 38-inch bust, and Uncle Wes said she had been the mistress of a gambling man before her marriage. Years after her death, when my brother researched the family tree, he found that she may also have been pregnant when she married Grandpa. Uncle Wes said he and his siblings always suspected that Dad had a different father from the rest of them, but he looked an awful lot like his dad to me.

I don't remember much about Grandpa Chamless, because by the time I was five or six years old, he and Grandma had separated, and Grandma had acquired the house in Springfield with the help of one of Dad's brothers, where she rented rooms to eke out a living. Dad said he was terribly upset when his parents got divorced, even though he was married and a father by then. I don't think it was the scandal that bothered him so much—or even the fact that he didn't see much of his father after that. I think it was because his dream of a loving, intact family had been severely damaged. Not that his dream ever had much basis in reality. It was just a romantic ideal he cherished.

Dad was always an idealist at heart, and despite his attempts to protect himself from his father's blows on that one occasion in his teens, he didn't seem to have a strong sense of self-preservation. Uncle Wes said that once a gang of boys was taunting Dad about being a goody-goody preacher's boy. They were trying to make him say "shit," and when he refused to do so, they began beating up on him. But he wouldn't fight back, either, so Uncle Wes had to jump in and rescue him. Although Wes was several years younger than Dad, he was even bigger and stronger— a virtual giant. When I was small, I saw him lift up the back of an automobile with his bare hands, which were the biggest I had ever seen. But despite his more self-protective instincts, he had a soft heart, like Dad. Mom said when Wes was living with her and Dad during their first year of marriage, he accidentally knocked a man out cold, after which he sat down on the curb and cried—a huge, husky teenager, sobbing like a baby. Most of Dad's siblings were like that—kind-hearted and good-natured like their mother. But, as in Mom's family, there was also a streak of violence on their father's side. When Dad got the genealogy bug in his fifties, he was devastated to discover that his paternal grandfather had killed his wife by hitting her in the head with a stick of firewood. I think Dad feared that the trait could be passed down in our genes, and he was passionately nonviolent.

All the kids in Dad's family had to work as soon as they were able, so Dad worked at a lot of jobs. He told me he once "pulled" 1,000 pounds of cotton in one day. Pulling cotton, he said, was quicker and easier than picking it, because you pulled the whole boll off the plant without separating it from the leaves, but 1,000 pounds was still an amazing amount to pull in one day, and he was kind of a local hero for a while. By the time he was 15, he went off to Lubbock, Texas, to work in a broom factory, giving Grandpa one less mouth to feed. The Assemblies of God pastor in Lubbock knew Grandpa and somehow assumed that Dad was a preacher, too, so one day, to Dad's astonishment, he announced that "Brother Paul is going to preach the sermon for us next Sunday." Dad had never preached a sermon in his life, but he didn't know how to say no, and preaching sounded like a better way to make a living than pulling cotton or working in a broom factory, so the next Sunday he found himself in the pulpit. That was his first step on the way to meeting the woman who would one day become my mom.

Dad was 21 and Mom was 23 when they met, but Dad had already been on the road for several years when he came to hold a revival for Mom in Paducah. Within a few months they were married in a "brush arbor"—a poor people's makeshift substitute for a tent—in Cairo, Illinois, during a revival Dad was holding. According to a newspaper clipping announcing the event, Dad's sermon that night was "The Citizens of Hell," a comically inappropriate subject for their wedding night, but an eerily prescient description of the state of our family life after we moved to Illinois. In the early days of their marriage, though, things were apparently good a lot of the time. During the first six years, Mom and Dad pastored churches in three Texas towns: Terrell, Highlands (where I was born), and Electra. The fact that they didn't stay in any place long might have indicated that they were both wanderers at heart. But throughout her time on the road and while we were in Waxahachie, Mom stayed in close touch with her mother. I still have a shoebox full of letters she wrote to her mother during those years before her return to Illinois, in which she provided detailed accounts of her life, down to how much she had paid for a pair of shoes.

It seemed to me that Mom was pretty happy during those years on the road and in Waxahachie, but she was drawn back to the bosom of her family to establish a permanent home. She purchased her security at a very high price, however: a reduction in her professional status, the loss of an independent income, and a serious curtailment of her social life. Throughout her life, Mom was a mass of contradictions, and while she never turned her back on her church, even when it betrayed her years later, she had never been as wholeheartedly conservative as many of its members. But as co-pastor of the church in East St. Louis, she was at the mercy of permanent congregational scrutiny. And now, because she and Dad owned a home for the first time in their lives—a home that her brothers had built—they could not pick up and move so easily as they had done before whenever they yearned for greener pastures.

In contrast to Mom's need to be surrounded by her family, Dad had no roots in a particular place and no intact family to which he longed to return. His mother was in Springfield, his dad was in San Angelo, Texas, and some of his siblings had already begun to spread out in different directions. So settling down in Collinsville was a profound change for him as well as for Mom, but in a different way. Not only was the move more permanent than any he had experienced in his life, but as the "outsider," he now had to compete with Mom's family for her attention and respect.

Although Dad was no stranger to hard work, he was a reader, a philosopher, and a dreamer at heart, and Mom couldn't help making invidious comparisons between him and her brothers, non-bookish types who worked outdoors in all kinds of weather, like her dad. Whenever Mom had a complaint about Dad, she could always run to her mother or her siblings, but Dad didn't have similar resources. "Your problem, Mary Ruth, is that you're overworked," was Grandma's frequent assessment of Mom's situation, which fed into Mom's lifelong sense of martyrdom.

Given the circumstances, it's not surprising that Dad spent long hours away from our home in Collinsville. It's also not surprising that Mom resented his absences and, considering Dad's good looks and what may or may not have happened in Waxahachie with the mysterious Violet, she began to suspect that he was fooling around. Grandpa's early abuse had probably convinced her that she was not pretty, and with no makeup and the severe hairstyle and loose-fitting clothing she wore as a preacher, she was definitely a brown wren beside Dad, who was movie-star handsome. She did have fabulous legs and a graceful way of moving, and people admired her musical talent, but most of them seemed more drawn to Dad.

Whether Dad was seeing other women during those early years in Collinsville, I never knew for sure, but I do know that after I was grown, when he and I were talking about a book we had both read—I think it was something by Aldous Huxley—Dad said, "There's a character in there who reminds me of myself." He didn't have to tell me which one it was; I instantly recognized him as the character who secretly rented a room in another part of town simply to have a place to get away from everybody.

While Mom and Dad were trying to adapt to John's birth and their new life in Illinois, I was also going through some major changes. I had to adjust to a new school and a neighborhood in which I was not the center of attention as I had been on the evangelistic field and at the Bible school in Texas. An added complication was that, shortly after my brother's birth, I began to experience the hormonal changes of puberty. Very soon, my breasts began to develop, and shortly after I turned eleven, I began menstruating. I also started getting interested in boys.

But before I became romantically interested in boys, I went through a period of being really angry with them. When I was in fourth grade, I started attacking them on the school playground. Once, when I tore a boy's shirt, he wore his jacket all afternoon, even though it was a hot day, so the teacher wouldn't see what I had done. A couple of weeks later, his mother invited me home for lunch with the boy and his little sister. Looking back, I'm struck by the graciousness of her effort to make peace between us. Her gentle method must have had good results because, as I recall, I behaved quite well at lunch and never beat up on her son again. After all, I didn't have anything against him personally. I was just mad at boys.

It never occurred to me back then that there could be any connection between my beating up boys at school and the introduction of a baby brother into my life. After all, I was totally devoted to John, doing my best to usurp Mom's role. In part, this role was forced upon me, as my parents had made me John's official babysitter almost from the day of his birth. But I was also genuinely attached to him, changing his diapers, comforting him when he was unhappy or sick, getting into the playpen to play with him and, when he was still a toddler, giving him rides in the basket of my bicycle. The summer he turned one year old, when I was approaching my tenth birthday, Dad had already taught me to drive our car, and by the time John was a preschooler, I was giving him and other children rides all over the neighborhood. Later, when I started dating, sometimes I took him along. If a boy didn't like my brother, that was a strike against him. I do have one indistinct, disturbing memory, though, of saying threatening things to my little brother when he was still an infant and I was babysitting him and feeling especially frustrated and unhappy. I don't remember what I said, but I do remember telling myself that he wouldn't understand it, so he couldn't be hurt by my words. I hope that's true.

Sometimes when I was left alone to care for John, I felt extremely stressed. More than once, my parents came home much later than expected. I didn't know where they were and I had no way to reach them, and I remember sobbing hysterically, wondering if they had been killed on the road somewhere or had decided to leave me and John behind, although when they finally arrived home, I didn't tell them how upset I had been. Looking back, I can recall other fears of abandonment. When John was still a preschooler and Mom started back to McKendree College to pursue her bachelor's degree, I remember watching out my bedroom window as she drove away in the early dawn and feeling a terrible sadness, as if she might never return. After my marriage, I experienced similar episodes of excruciating anxiety when my sportswriter husband, who worked nights, did not come home at the expected hour.

But despite these anxieties, I always felt older and more mature than my peers when I was growing up. Not only had my parents treated me almost like an adult in many ways, but on the road and at the college I had been around adults or teenagers much more often than children, so my self-concept was somewhat skewed. Only when Mom was angry with me did she resort to treating me like a child and, unused to such treatment, I found it very hard to take. She had never trained me to say "yes ma'am" and "no ma'am" to adults—except when she was angry. Then, in the middle of a fierce tirade, she would force me to say "yes ma'am," and the words would stick in my throat as I tried to hold back my tears. I must admit that I wasn't always meek in these encounters, although I never dared to shout at my mother or be openly defiant. But by imitation, I had learned the art of sarcasm very early, and I sometimes used it at my peril with the person from whom I had learned it. Many times I felt the unanticipated sting of a sharp slap across my face for something I had said. Sometimes I wonder if my lifelong anxiety about tornadoes, plane crashes and other sudden disasters may be a kind of PTSD from those attacks that often seemed to come out of nowhere. I was more afraid of my mother than of any other living being, so as life became more difficult for me at home, I began to smart off at school, arguing with my teachers and sometimes even correcting their mistakes.

Even then, though, I was aware at some level that my misbehavior at school was not really directed at my teachers. I actually loved school and didn't dislike any of the teachers, but I could vent my anger with them more safely than with Mom. I think some of them may have suspected there was more to my smart remarks than met the eye, because one time when I returned to school after my private piano lesson while the other students were still out on the playground, my teacher said, "Pat, I wouldn't mind some of the things you say if you just wouldn't say them in front of the other students."

In my encounters with Mom, though, she held all the cards, and she always won. She was not above taunting me with her superior power, either. When I was older, she liked to tell a story about an incident that happened in my early teens. Mom and I had been standing with some other women in the back of the church and she was trying, with what I regarded as a poor attempt at subtlety, to persuade me to do something or other that I didn't want to do. In her telling of the story, I said, rather snottily, "Why don't you try using psychology on me?" After I left, she said one of the women had remarked, "If any child has ever had psychology used on her, it's Pat." This was the kind of mind game that Mom was really good at. As far as I was aware back then, she had *never* used psychology on me—she had simply told me what to do and I obeyed, or I resisted her orders and suffered the consequences. So when she told me others could see that I had been manipulated by her clever psychology, I was completely thrown off balance, as she knew I would be. Checkmate. Game to Mom.

The growing rift with my mother and my erroneous belief that I was mature beyond my years both contributed to my precocious involvement in sex. And there was another factor that, I suspect, played a role: my reading. One thing I have always appreciated about my parents is that both of them loved to read and never restricted my reading in any way. But that uncensored reading, in the context of my mother's frequent accusations that Dad was having affairs and my dad's interest in the psychology of human sexual behavior, may also have helped to direct my thoughts in ways that were not the best for my age. In fact, an objective observer might have felt that the air in our house fairly crackled with sex, although mostly in a negative way. Dad had told me where babies come from when I was only five years old (I learned years later that Mom resented his usurping what she thought should have been her role). And by the time I reached puberty, having perused medical texts containing graphic illustrations of childbirth, *Coronet* magazines with arty black-and-white photos of nudes, books on human sexuality by authors like Havelock Ellis, and novels in which many of the characters engaged in premarital or extramarital sex, I was almost certainly over-stimulated.

In contrast to my dad's liberal view of sexuality, my mother clearly harbored some feelings that the whole subject was dirty, and she did her best to inculcate that attitude in me. She had a unique knack of making a word sound incredibly nasty, including the word "stupid," which she applied to any activity or person of whom she disapproved, and there was something about the way she pronounced "sex," slurring the "s" and stretching out the one-syllable word, that made me feel dirty even at the sound of it. The summer after my brother's birth, she pulled me aside for a serious talk. I no longer would be allowed to wear shorts, she said, because I was becoming a woman. "How would you feel," she asked, "if I paraded around the yard in my underwear?" The comparison didn't make sense to me, but I knew better than to argue, so when I rode my bike to the school playgrounds on weekends to play softball with my girlfriends, I hid a pair of shorts in my bag and changed when I got to school.

More damaging, I think, was the aftermath of an incident that happened while I was home babysitting John when he was about two years old. By this time, my inclination to beat up on boys had begun to morph into more amorous aspirations, and Jimmy, a new blonde, blue-eyed boy in the neighborhood, had caught my eye. Somehow, one warm summer evening, he ended up on my front porch, where we spent the evening hugging and kissing in full view of the neighbors while my toddler brother was left largely to his own devices. When my parents got home, Mom was furious to find that the dishes were still undone, and the next day she got an earful from the neighbors about what I had been doing when I should have been washing the dishes and taking care of my brother. The tongue-lashing I got from her that day made me feel so disgusted and ashamed that I was never able to speak to that boy again or even look him in the eye.

In the end, however, Mom's lectures and warnings served only to help drive me into sexual activity long before I was prepared to deal with it.

"Uncle Wes, how come all the Chamlesses are oversexed?" my cousin Cheryl joked with Dad's brother when she and I were both middle-aged. There was more than a grain of truth in her observation, so perhaps it's unfair to put all the blame for my precocious sexuality on the atmosphere in my home and the growing hostility between my mother and me. Some of it may have been purely genetic. My paternal grandmother was quite the femme fatale in her day, and her six beautiful daughters, to whom men were drawn like bees to flowers, had obviously inherited her sparkle. And Grandpa Chamless, over six feet tall and confidently sporting the Stetson hat so popular in Texas, was surely no slouch himself to have won my grandmother's hand in marriage. So I may have come by my early interest in sex naturally, although I think romance and a need for love were as big a part of it as sex.

For many years, I thought no one in my dad's family knew about my teenage pregnancy, but Dad's sisters always seemed eager to help me find a boyfriend. One incident in particular stands out. It happened when I went to spend the night with Aunt Wanda Fay in her high-rise apartment building on Delmar Avenue in St. Louis. Voluptuous and fun loving, she was a manicurist at the exclusive Missouri Athletic Club, where I concluded that she was very popular with its rich members, since her apartment was full of gifts they had given her. I was enchanted by her glamour and thrilled to be spending the evening in her company. Dad's sisters were never shy about making conversation with strangers, and that night when Aunt Wanda Fay took me to dinner at the popular Parkmoor Restaurant on Clayton Road, there were soon three or four young men hanging around our booth, making conversation. During a ladies room break, my aunt told me we should wait until they left before going to her car, but when we finally went out to the parking lot, there they were, waiting. They followed us home and into the lobby of her apartment building, but she refused to get into the elevator until they had left.

My parents' attitudes toward sex were very different, as were their attitudes toward nudity and modesty. While Mother never, ever, walked around the house in her slip, Dad's family was much more casual about such things. In fact, there was a funny story about the time Uncle Wes, frustrated because his baby sister, Billie Jo, had lingered in the tub too long, broke down the bathroom door and started shaving while she was still bathing. So I guess it shouldn't be surprising that after we moved to Belleville, I began to notice my dad walking around the house in his white cotton briefs. Had he always done so and I just noticed it because the one-story floor plan of our new house made it more likely that he would stroll past my room half-naked? Or was I just now noticing it because I was becoming more sexually aware? Or—a more disturbing thought—was he unconsciously stimulated by my emerging sexuality and indulging in male preening?

When I was growing up, even after I was a teenager, Dad often got into bed with me in the morning to talk. My little brother occasionally slept all night with me until I went away to college, and it all seemed perfectly natural to me at the time. I'm sure there are lots of families in which this kind of behavior would seem out of line, and, in fact, I learned after I was grown that Mom had been disturbed about Dad's getting into bed with me in the morning. But he never touched me inappropriately or made suggestive remarks. And while his keen interest in the psychology of human sexuality was a matter of common knowledge, he never showed the least interest in dirty jokes, off-color conversation, or sexist attitudes toward women. While I can't totally eliminate the possibility that Dad was acting out unconscious desires, I believe it is equally likely that, crazy as I was about my dad, I was more aware of his semi-nudity because of my own sexual awakening. It is certainly no accident, though, that the boy I fell in love with looked so much like my daddy.

Whether my interest in sex was genetic, environmental, or a combination of factors, it began to be obvious while I was still very young, like the time when I was about eleven years old and spent the night with a girlfriend from church. She and her good-looking brother Chuck, two or three years older than I, had bedrooms in the attic, separated only by a curtain. That night as I lay in bed on the other side of the curtain, I began carrying on a flirtatious banter with Chuck across the room. After awhile, I got up and walked to stand just inside the curtain, striking my most provocative pose in my shorty pajamas with the halter top. Soon Chuck came over to his sister's side of the attic and sat on the bed, hugging and kissing me. He may have touched my breasts, but nothing more untoward happened. I remember thinking, though, as I put my arms around him, "This is like hugging my daddy." From my first sexual experience, I was never able to find a clear demarcation between sex and affection. For me, sex was then—and throughout most of my life it remained—not only a means of physical gratification and validation of my attractiveness; it was also inseparable from romance and my need for love. I suspect that's true of a lot of girls who end up getting pregnant as teenagers. Chuck was a real charmer who attracted not only girls, but also their mothers. In fact, he and my mother eventually forged a friendship that lasted throughout the rest of her life. But by the time I was approaching 13, I had my eye on another boy.

Six years older than I, Ronnie was, superficially, almost the spitting image of my daddy: tall, dark, and handsome. His widowed mother was a member of our church, but I didn't know him well because his attendance was irregular. One night after church, however, I saw my chance, and I struck. I was standing on the front porch of our little white frame church with a bunch of kids when I turned to Ronnie and asked, "How's my boyfriend?"

With a somewhat puzzled look, he replied, "I don't know. Who is he?"

Giving my best imitation of a vamp, I replied throatily, "You are."

I don't recall exactly what happened next. All I know is that soon Ronnie and I were part of a group of kids and young adults from church who went skating on Tuesday nights at the roller rink in Troy, Illinois, where I discovered that Ronnie was, as they say now, "all that and a bag of chips." He was an exceptionally graceful skater who could do the waltz with a partner and skate backwards, two things I never learned to do. I soon discovered that he was also a very good swimmer and diver. By that time, most of the people in our church had relaxed their objections to mixed bathing, so after awhile we all started going swimming together at the Turner Pool in Belleville, where I watched with undisguised admiration as he did graceful dives off the high board. I was enchanted, and proud to be his girlfriend. Sometimes I took John along when we went swimming, and once Ronnie took him on a camping trip. The way he treated my little brother made me love him all the more.

At first, we kids went on these outings as a group, five or six in one car. But before long, Ronnie and I started going for rides in his car, accompanied only by a friend Ronnie referred to as "Jackson," as if he were our chauffeur, although his real name was Richard. Richard was either a little slow or terribly shy and lonely, or both, because he didn't seem to mind driving Ronnie's second-hand black Pontiac with the steeply sloping back all around town while Ronnie and I were in the back seat making out. By the time I was thirteen, we were making love every chance we got—at his aunt's house, at mine when my parents were away, outside at night, and even in his bedroom once. That time, his mother came home and almost caught us. She figured out what was going on and tore into him, embarrassing me to death, but she didn't tell my parents.

To this day, I can't explain why my parents let me date at such a young age—especially with a boy so much older than I. What is even more puzzling is they had plenty of hints that we were becoming intimate, and Mom, at least, was clearly upset about it. Once she remarked with disapproval, "People say you two act like a married couple." Another time, she gave me a tongue-lashing for sitting on Ronnie's lap in public. On still another occasion, she was very disturbed to find a bunch of cash hidden in a book on my shelf. Having dropped out of school, Ronnie had a job loading boxcars down at the railroad yards in East St. Louis, and he was making pretty good money for a young man without much education, but he showed no interest in literature or learning. In fact, one time he told me "You think too much"—a charge I was to hear from many people over the years. But he was trying to save up for our future, and he had given the money to me for safekeeping. Mom was scandalized when she discovered I was taking money from him. (In my mind, it was about $200, but it could have been considerably less.) She was also upset when he gave me an opal ring for my fourteenth birthday, but she didn't make me give it back, to my great relief.

The worst thing, though, was the time she caught us necking in the living room one evening. With a scowl that would scorch paint, she sent him home, took me in the bedroom, and beat me with a belt, declaring, "I'm going to make a lady out of you or kill you!" After she had vented her fury and left the room, I crawled out the window, walked several miles down the dark road from Signal Hill Boulevard that crossed over Illinois Highway 157 into the narrow streets of East St. Louis to Ronnie's house, where I threw rocks at his window until he came outside. Not knowing what else to do, he took me back home. I don't remember what happened when I got there, but that's probably a blessing.

In contrast to Mom's behavior, Dad took me aside late one evening and told me he suspected I was having sex with Ronnie. "Be discreet, Honey," he told me. I didn't tell him that I didn't even know the meaning of the word, although I recognized his gesture as a warning to be careful. Discretion, however, was never one of the items in my personal toolkit—and still isn't, I fear.

I told myself what Ronnie and I were doing was OK because we were in love and were going to marry someday, but against that rationalization were stacked all the sermons I had heard over the years, along with the warnings about inappropriate behavior from my mother. I constantly vacillated between feeling like a romantic heroine from a novel and, on the other hand, the vilest kind of sinner. What's worse, sometimes when Ronnie and I were making love, I thought, "If only Mom knew," and the idea gave me a delicious feeling of revenge. So when the world came crashing down around our whole family's ears a year or so after the abortion, I shouldered a load of guilt that would dog me throughout most of the rest of my life.

"If you've got anything to do, do it in the dark," my grandmother had said to Mom when she was growing up. This advice, which my mother repeated to me, seemed to me not only hypocritical, but almost sinister. I guess Mom took it to heart, though, because when she was in her 80s, she told me, "There are things I will carry with me to my grave." Part of her behavior was simply "keeping up a front," which most families of her generation tried to do, I think. But from some of the things she said, I also believe her tendency to keep secrets was more than mere hypocrisy. I think her philosophy was that human failings should be hidden to avoid providing a bad example for others. In contrast, I have always believed that it's better to know and deal with the truth, insofar as that's possible. To this day, I'm not sure which of us was right.

During those turbulent years, I knew, of course, that Mom was attending college part-time, running a household, raising two children, co-pastoring a church, helping to produce a weekly radio program and teaching school. What I didn't know was that she was also helping to deal with a lot of other problems in her extended family. For example, a decade after Mom's death I discovered I had a close relative I had never met. It turned out that one of Mom's family members who owned a nursing home had gotten one of his young employees pregnant. He was married and had several children to support. Moreover, the girl was African American, and most of Mom's family, while not obsessed with race, was nowhere near prepared to accept the idea of sex between the races. I had always known that around that time, this relative had experienced some business reverses and lost everything. He didn't declare bankruptcy but spent about 20 years trying to climb out of the hole, during which time Mom was giving a few dollars every month "to help pay off his dairy bills from the nursing home." After my brother and I discovered our long-lost relative—or, rather, his wife found us on Facebook—we speculated, through a bit of sleuthing, that what Mom actually had been doing was giving money to help with the baby's care. In her convoluted way of obscuring the truth without lying, Mom could tell herself that she *really was* "helping to pay off the dairy bill from the nursing home."

Wherever she could, Mom provided financial help, moral support, and actual physical labor to friends and family members during times of crisis. Sometimes I felt as if I weren't a bona fide member of her family, though, because, while I occasionally got hints of something going on, there were several secrets that I didn't learn about until years later. And I'm pretty sure there are more that I will never know.

Of course I had some secrets of my own back then. For the first few weeks after the abortion, I was still in shock. I was humiliated and embarrassed. I didn't know what to say to the students and teachers when I went back to school or to my friends at church. I longed to see Ronnie, to whom I had been forbidden to speak, and I mourned the loss of our baby. But life seems to have infinite room for all kinds of activities and emotions when one is young, and somehow I got through it all, continuing to do well in all of my classes and even playing my flute in the school orchestra. Usually, I rode the bus home from school, which was about three miles from our house, but on nice days, sometimes I walked with a couple of girls from my neighborhood, stopping at a little grocery store on the way home to get Hostess cupcakes or soda pop.

One day as we were walking, a familiar black Pontiac with a sloping back pulled to the curb and stopped beside us. "Pat," Ronnie called from inside. Throwing aside my fears and the dire warnings from my parents, I got in.

By that time, Mom had obtained her bachelor's degree from McKendree College and was teaching school in East St. Louis, so she got home even later than I did. So Ronnie and I had a precious half hour or more to be together after school whenever he didn't have to work. He would pick me up a few blocks from the school and drive around as long as we dared and then drop me off a few blocks from home so I could keep up the pretext of walking home. He wanted to know what had happened after our return from Arkansas, and, despite the warnings from my parents, I told him everything.

For a while, our contact was limited to those short afternoon rides—until Ronnie started coming to my window at night. Our house on Signal Hill Boulevard had a walk-out basement, and Mom and Dad's bedroom was at the back, over the garage, but my room was toward the front, where the ground was high enough under my window that Ronnie could speak to me through the screen by stretching a bit. There was a narrow strip of grass between our house and the one next door where "Miss Alexander," an elderly spinster lived, and the area was sheltered by tall hedges on her side, so it was a pretty safe place for us to meet. Kissing and touching hands through the screen, we would talk for hours. Once I even unhooked the screen and crawled out the window to go for a middle-of-the-night ride with my young lover, but I was so fearful of being caught that I became hysterical and he had to bring me back home, boosting me up to crawl back into the security of my bedroom.

Like a modern-day Romeo and Juliet, we met this way for months, even into the following summer before my 16th birthday. That was when my mother encouraged me to lie about my age to get a full-time job as a collator in the credit office of Famous-Barr department store in St. Louis, where her sister Edith was a biller. I'm sure Mom thought that having a job would help to take my mind off Ronnie. I had to be at work early in the morning, and the bus ride through East St. Louis and across the Mississippi took close to an hour each way, so I left early each morning and didn't get home until suppertime. Several years later, Mom told me she used to go over to Famous-Barr and take the escalator from the eighth floor, where the credit offices were, to the ninth floor so she could look over the office walls, which didn't reach to the ceiling, and watch me work. She said she felt sorry for me because I looked so tired, but what she didn't know was that I was tired from staying up half the night talking to Ronnie.

On a few occasions, I managed to sneak Ronnie into the house when my parents and John were out. At those times we made love, as we did in the car whenever we had a chance, and our only method of birth control was still withdrawal. I guess we thought carrying condoms would be an admission of intent. Or maybe Ronnie just didn't like them. And if I had known how to get any, I would have been far too embarrassed to try. I still couldn't get up the nerve to buy my own Kotex.

I still loved and wanted Ronnie, but I was also wracked by guilt and shame, not to mention a terror of getting pregnant again. After one of those lovemaking sessions when no one was home, I remember standing in front of my mother's full-length mirror telling my reflection, over and over, "I hate you, I hate you," as, once again, the tears streamed down my face.

During the time that Ronnie and I were meeting clandestinely, my parents tried to dissuade me from dwelling on the romance by hinting that Ronnie was dating other girls. "Someone saw Ronnie and Jeannie driving together in his car the other day," one of them said. Jeannie, the soprano in our trio, was two years older than I and kind of a Marilyn Monroe wannabe, so that was disturbing news. I'm sure my parents were hoping to convince me that Ronnie was not waiting for me and, therefore, I should not wait for him. But my reaction was to feel even more insecure. Could I trust anybody? Were they lying, or was he really forgetting about me?

So I began to doubt. I was still in my mid-teens, and as much as I loved Ronnie, I was getting restless, weary of having to steal half an hour with him after school or talk to him through my window screen at night when I had to get up early the next day. College was only two years away, and I began to envy the others girls who had boyfriends, and dates. I felt like Rapunzel, locked in a tower because of my love for someone who might not even be true to me. So I started to draw away from Ronnie, and when I did, he decided to fight back by telling our secrets. I imagine he felt he had been wronged—after all, he had been prepared to marry me, and Mom and Dad had kept him from doing so. Worse still, they had forced me to get rid of his child. Probably he wanted them to pay for what they had done.

And pay they would. As would I.

Within a year after my abortion, our church began to fall apart. There is usually at least one person in every congregation who likes to stir up trouble and is eagerly awaiting the chance to rally a critical mass of indignant parishioners to his or her cause. Eventually, someone in our church began trying to win the support of others to confront my parents about the story that was making the rounds. Soon there were little clusters of people huddled together after church, talking in low tones and casting furtive glances at us. Word of all this got back to us, of course, and in my eyes, Ronnie became the enemy and my chief betrayer.

I was growing scared, and so were my parents. One of my most painful memories of that time is of trying to calm my mother as she walked down our boulevard in her housecoat late at night, crying and half out of her mind with fear. I was also very proud and a little surprised when my dad bravely preached a sermon against carrying tales, as everyone in the congregation knew who and what he was talking about.

At the end of our church services, there was often an "altar call," in which sinners were invited to come forward and accept Christ as their personal savior or "backsliders" were encouraged to come and "get right with God." During this sometimes prolonged period, Mom played the piano while the congregation slowly sang "Softly and tenderly Jesus is calling, calling for you and for me . . ." while waiting for sinners to come and fall on their knees at the altar that ran across the front of the church, begging for forgiveness. After the self-confessed sinners had come forward, a general altar call was issued, in which all the faithful were invited to come and pray with them or just "have a little talk with Jesus," as one popular quartet number described it. During this period, I spent a lot of time on my knees at the altar, silently but tearfully praying for God's forgiveness while entreating him not to rain down his wrath upon my parents and me.

One night at the height of the whispering campaign, I lingered on my knees long after services had effectively ended, and as I finally rose and turned around, I saw Ronnie and some of his supporters standing at the back of the pews, near the entrance, clearly poised for a showdown. Terrified, I hurried over to my friend Faye for help. She was a young mother who had attended the Bible school in Waxahachie when we were there, and she and her husband had bought our house in Collinsville when we moved to Belleville the summer before my freshman year of high school. Although she was 13 years older than I, we had become close friends. Seeing Ronnie staring at me with a menacing look, we rushed out the door beside the altar and jumped in her car, hoping to avoid confrontation.

The only thing I could think to do was ask Faye to drive to Uncle Jim's house in Collinsville, more than seven miles away. In addition to being a carpenter, Uncle Jim was an amateur gymnast and weightlifter. I had heard that his cousin Reggie, who had just gotten out of jail for some unspecified act of violence, was currently staying at his house. So during our wild chase down Illinois Highway 157 with Ronnie's Pontiac in hot pursuit, I was praying that the two men could scare Ronnie and his friends off.

When we got there, we leaned on the horn and the two men came out of the house to see what was the matter. I don't remember anything about what happened next, except that I managed to avoid a confrontation with Ronnie. Never in my wildest dreams could I have imagined, then, that Ronnie and Uncle Jim would become friends nearly half a century later, but as I was to learn again and again over the years, life is full of surprises.

Soon our worst fears were realized when Mom, Dad and I were called for questioning before a group of Assemblies of God officials. These officials, called "district presbyters," were responsible, among other things, for ensuring that the ministers of each congregation did not stray from the fold. When the denomination was first established in the early 1900s, it was envisioned as a loose affiliation between Pentecostal congregations. Unlike churches with more centralized organizational structures, it was an association of semi-autonomous congregations, or "assemblies," answerable to but one authority: God. For that reason, the leaders preferred to call themselves a "movement," rather than a denomination. Despite their extremely loose structure, however, they soon recognized the need for a minimal central authority that would handle official publications, keep congregations in touch with one another, and provide for the official ordination of ministers. So the country was divided into districts, each represented by a group of presbyters who were, themselves, ministers.

In the early decades of the movement, there were no educational or gender restrictions on candidates for the ministry. As far as I could tell, the only requirements were that candidates should have a familiarity with the King James Bible, be of good moral character, and confirm that they had been "born again," baptized by immersion, and "filled with the Holy Spirit," as evidenced by "speaking in tongues." If these requirements were met and the presbyters were convinced that the candidate had a "calling" from God, he or she would be ordained. But if serious charges—criminal, moral, or doctrinal—were brought against a minister, the presbyters also had the power to examine the charges and, if they deemed the action appropriate, revoke ordination.

In the middle of all the gossip at our church, someone had brought charges against my parents, and so it was that sometime after my 16th birthday, we found ourselves riding to Springfield for a hearing before the presbyters.

All my life I have believed that the hearing was in Springfield, Illinois, a couple of hours' drive from our home in Belleville, but the current Illinois headquarters are not in Springfield but in Carlinville, so now I am wondering if we drove the 250 miles to the national headquarters in Springfield, Missouri. The fact that I have no memory of those drives to and from the hearing gives some indication of my state of abject terror during that awful time. While certain aspects of the experience are seared on my brain, others have been totally blacked out.

I can imagine, though, some of the things that were going through our minds during that drive. No doubt each of us was visualizing a bleak future for the family. Mom, at least, had her teaching certificate and a stable job with the East St. Louis school district, but Dad, with no education and no job experience beyond preaching since the age of 15, had only his income from selling used books to fall back on, and that was certainly not enough to provide a living even for him, let alone for the family.

Moreover, our whole lives were tied up in the church. Virtually all of our friends, locally and around the country, as well as many family members on both sides, belonged to the Assemblies of God. To lose their papers and be objects of scandal within the church would be the worst kind of exile for my parents. I don't think anyone ever mentioned prison, which was too horrible even to think about.

Since I can recall nothing of it, I assume that the trip was almost totally silent. What I do know is that my parents did not tell me what to say if I were questioned. Maybe, like me, they were making promises to God and praying for a miracle. I had already seen the paralyzing fear that my reckless acts had engendered in my parents, and, what's worse, I realized with sudden clarity that they didn't have any idea what to do in the face of this calamity.

In childhood, we tend to think of our parents as all-powerful, but now I saw that they were only human, and I could not escape the knowledge that all this terror and heartbreak was the result, at least in part, of my desire to get back at my mother for what I had perceived as her mistreatment of me. Unfortunately, I had succeeded beyond my wildest expectations. "Don't get yourself talked about," she had told me many times in my short life. Now all the people of our church—even at the level of the presbyters—seemed to be talking about nothing else.

I felt terribly sorry for Mom but even worse for Dad, who, except for the couple of times he had lost his temper during Mom's postpartum breakdown, had been the most loving, caring parent any child could ask for, even if he was distracted and absent-minded at times. Mom had told me more than once that, on the day I was born in that little house in Highlands, he had declared happily, "I like little girls!" And, as he himself told me, he had immediately taken me from the doctor's hands to examine every inch of my body to ensure that I was whole. The only flaw he could find, he said, was on my left ear. Where the top rolls over to form a kind of cuff, the skin had fused with the part of the ear behind it. Throughout my growing-up years, he would occasionally push my hair aside tenderly and check to see if that part of my ear was still fused. I loved my daddy with all my heart, and now I was about to ruin his life.

When we finally arrived at the headquarters in Springfield, Dad went in alone at first, leaving Mom and me in the car. But soon he came back to say that the presbyters wanted to speak to me alone.

Looking back on that time, I have often thought of the story of "Susanna and the Elders," in the 13th chapter of the book of Daniel. Susanna, the beautiful and virtuous daughter of a wealthy man, had unwittingly become the object of lust for two dirty old men, Jewish elders with the power to adjudicate disputes in their community. The two men had hidden in the bushes to spy on her while she was bathing. But of course my story was very different from hers. I knew I was guilty as charged, and those presbyters were just doing their jobs. Nevertheless, I felt as naked as Susanna had been on that day when she bathed unaware that she was being watched by two lustful old men. What was worse, I knew that my parents' fate was in my hands.

"You understand why you are here, don't you?" the lead interrogator asked, to which I answered yes.

"You understand that God is watching, and that he knows if you are telling the truth, don't you?" he continued, to which I again answered yes.

Lying has never come easily to me. In all the time I had been intimate with Ronnie and sneaked around to see him, I had desperately tried to avoid lies of commission. Lies of omission, of course, were another story. Perhaps I had unconsciously learned indirection from my mother. What my parents didn't know couldn't hurt me, I thought, and I had become very adept at diverting attention from anything that might arouse their suspicion and omitting all information that might give me away. But outright lying had never been my style, and it still isn't. When I was young, I thought I would be risking hellfire, and although my fear of hellfire has long since faded into obscurity, I still don't feel right about lying, except to save a life.

I have always been suspicious of memoirs in which long conversations are quoted verbatim, so I readily admit that I don't remember the men's exact words during that hearing. But I remember that I lied.

They asked me if I had undergone an abortion, and I said no.

They asked me if I had ever had sexual relations with Ronnie, and I said no.

They asked me how I could explain some of the things I had written in letters to Ronnie while I was on vacation at Ray's in Texas that summer before my 15th birthday. They had my letters, they informed me, and the letters seemed to indicate an intimate relationship between the two of us.

I don't know what I said in response, except that I continued to deny that we had been intimate.

And then they asked an unexpected question: "If none of these things happened, why do you think he would make such a charge, and where would he get such an idea?"

Some readers may consider me sacrilegious for saying so, but I can only attribute my answer to divine inspiration. "I guess he's mad at me for not being his girlfriend anymore," I replied. "He told me that his brother's wife had an operation like that, so maybe that's where he got the idea."

I'm not sure when Ronnie had told me his brother's wife's had undergone an abortion—probably during the time we were meeting secretly and discussing what had happened—but my unrehearsed answer was apparently what made the presbyters begin to question the charges against us, or at least doubt that they were going to get any more useful information out of me, because soon afterwards they told me to go out to the car and send my dad in.

Dad didn't know, of course, what I had told the presbyters, nor did Mom, and as we sat in the car anxiously awaiting Dad's return, she didn't ask. What I will never forget, though, is the expression on Dad's face when he came back a short time later—a look of both amazement and relief, as if a great weight had been suddenly and unexpectedly lifted from his shoulders.

"She denied everything," he said.

Although we got a brief reprieve on that day, there were still many trials ahead for our family. Apparently, there was at least one subsequent hearing that I didn't learn about until later, in which my mother had to defend her own character. In an effort to comfort me immediately after my abortion, Mom had told me that she had undergone an experience similar to mine in her youth, but the baby had died, and she didn't offer any further details. However, during the hearings, her effort to comfort me came back to haunt her. I had shared my mom's secret with Ronnie, and, evidently, he had shared it with someone else. But sometime after my encounter with the presbyters, Mom informed me that the woman in whose home she and Dad had spent their wedding night had testified that their bed sheets had been bloody—proof of Mom's virginity before marriage. This new information confused me, since I couldn't figure out if Mom had lied to me before or was lying to me now. But I didn't dare ask.

Something else was going on behind the scenes during that time, too—something I could never even begin to figure out until many years later. And even now, I can only speculate about the meaning of it all. What I do know is that on another day, after my hearing before the presbyters, I again found myself in the car with my parents—this time on the way to the office of a prominent East St. Louis attorney named Dan McGlynn, who was reputed to be the Republican boss of the corrupt St. Clair County, Illinois, which encompassed both East St. Louis and Belleville. Local rumor back then was that, by a gentlemen's agreement,

McGlynn divided his turf with the Democratic county sheriff, whose name I have since forgotten. Mom's family had some strong Republican ties, so for a long time I assumed that Uncle Bill had put Mom in touch with McGlynn, but in doing some research for this part of my story, I also discovered that McGlynn's firm had represented Keeley Brothers Contracting Company, for which my grandpa was foreman, so perhaps Grandpa had a hand in the matter. I never had the slightest indication that he knew anything about what was going on, but my mother's family was full of secrets, so I will never know for sure.

In any case, I was once again sent to meet an interrogator in private, and, as my parents had done before the hearing with the presbyters, they didn't tell me what to say. But somehow I sensed that this situation was different. I was a good student and an avid reader, so I knew that attorneys couldn't tell anyone what you told them. I also knew that, in order to defend a client, an attorney had to know everything. So I told him the truth. Everything.

And that was the end of it.

I was never told the reason for this visit or what happened as a result. I always assumed that it had to do with possible slander charges, but many years later, something Dad said made a light bulb go on in my head: ". . . intimidating that poor widow woman," he had said in recalling our long-ago troubles. It dawned on me then that perhaps McGlynn had been hired to frighten Ronnie's mother into backing off from her claims by threatening a charge of statutory rape against her son, or even kidnapping, if she continued to insist that he had been intimate with me. After all, when we had run away, I was only 14 and Ronnie was 20, and by the time the issue was taken to the presbyters, I was somewhere around 16 and Ronnie 22. Could that have been the case? I will never know.

Half a century later I would learn that Dad had been ambivalent from the beginning about sending me for an abortion. Despite all the troubles Ronnie and his mother caused us, he had always felt some compassion for them. Perhaps he was remembering his own youth as a poor, uneducated young man in love.

Having failed to get my parents defrocked, the opposing faction in our church continued to spread rumors and accusations. Our once-happy congregation, which had always welcomed sinners, rejoiced in their rehabilitation and embraced them as part of the church family, became more like a pit of vipers, striking out at one another and forgetting all about God's message of love that Dad had tried so hard to instill. Things finally got so bad that Dad decided to call for a vote of confidence.

At its height, the membership rolls at Bethel Tabernacle on 84th Street in East St. Louis had probably never contained more than 200 names, and attendance had topped out at around 125, hovering nearer to 100 most of the time. But during all the strife, attendance had fallen off sharply. No one could be blamed for not wanting to come to a church where the atmosphere was so toxic and completely counter to all of Christ's teachings.

Still, Mom and Dad had a loyal core of supporters who attended faithfully, week after week, keeping our family going through the tithes and offerings they put in the plate on Sundays. I suspect some of them had their doubts about where the truth actually lay—it would be hard not to, especially since I had told some of my girlfriends in the church about being intimate with Ronnie. But our supporters were the kind of Christians who focused on Jesus' admonition to "judge not, lest ye be judged," and they put God's love into practice.

An awful lot of people in today's world who brandish the "Christian" label don't seem to remember Christ's teaching in the Sermon on the Mount, but those who stood by our family in our distress are a permanent reminder to me that there have always been some true Christians in the world, and because of what happened during that time, I have come to the conclusion that while religion can make good people better, it can also make bad people worse. It's human nature, I think, to find in your religion the justification for being the kind of person you are already inclined to be.

On the day of the vote of confidence, people who hadn't shown their faces in years were suddenly very concerned about the sanctity of the leadership of God's House. Extra chairs had to be set up in the back of the little church to accommodate everyone. Although it should have been like Old Home Week with all the lost sheep returning to the fold, the atmosphere was tense as the deacons checked each name off the roll and handed out ballots. Mom and Dad were grim-faced, and I was petrified to be at the center of this storm. What would we do if the people threw us out? How could I ever forgive myself? And could my parents ever forgive me?

My little brother, who was six and seven years old during this period, must have felt the tension, too, and I'm pretty sure he failed to receive all the attention he deserved during my parents' frantic attempts to keep us afloat, but it would be years before he learned the details of all that had been going on. I know something about how the subsequent changes in our family life affected his later years, but I will never know what emotional impact all of it had on him at the time of the abortion and the church breakup, and I doubt if he knows himself. It was just one more thing I had on my conscience. In fact, after my return from the unsuccessful elopement, Mom told me that I had promised to take John somewhere after school that day, and he had sat on the front stoop of our house for several hours waiting for me. The thought of my poor little brother waiting in vain for me to keep my promise never failed to fill me with guilt and remorse. I am somewhat comforted now when he tells me that he doesn't remember the incident, but the image of betraying my little brother haunted me for a long, long time.

When the ballots were counted, our side won by a narrow margin. I never learned the exact count, but it was apparently a secure enough margin that those who had voted against us decided to take their revenge by withdrawing their membership and joining other congregations in the area. In at least one case, a brother and sister split their loyalties, with the sister and her family transferring membership, while the brother and his family stuck with us. With the dissenters gone, though, attendance dwindled to a handful of people, perhaps 60 on good days. One of the many things that made me feel so guilty was the thought that our income from the church had been cut in half, since my parents, who had never been on salary, were dependent on the offering plate, but Dad told me later that some of the more loyal members had stepped up and increased their contributions. So the drop in our income was not as severe as it might have been. I don't know who those people were, and I'm sure they are all dead by now, but they have my eternal gratitude.

For a few months after the vote of confidence, our little church struggled on while my parents tried to figure out whether they could revive the ailing congregation or should leave and let someone else have a go at it. During that time, Dad brought in a number of visiting preachers, trying to see who might be the best candidate to take over and bring the church back to life. Eventually, he decided to throw his support behind a young man who had been a guest in the pulpit several times and whose wife—like Mom, and like so many other ministers' wives in the Assemblies of God—played the piano. Encouraged by Dad's support, the members who had remained with the church elected this couple to lead the congregation, and Dad and Mom stepped down a few months before I headed off to college at Oklahoma State University.

Until I left for college, Mom and I continued to attend Bethel Tabernacle, but Dad went on the road as a fundraiser for the Assemblies of God-supported Evangel College in Springfield, Missouri. From what I heard, he was very successful as a fundraiser, and he later told me that while I was away studying architecture during my freshman year at Oklahoma State, he and Mom had briefly rekindled their romance after years of bickering. They always got along better when there was some space between them, and perhaps the fact that I was gone helped, as well.

But after about a year, Dad grew weary of spending so many nights on the road, giving his pitch for the college to congregations all over the Midwest, so he decided to come home and try to make a living selling books. He set up a used bookstore called Landmark Gallery on 10th Street in East St. Louis and hired me to work there in the summer between my freshman and sophomore years. Unfortunately, the store was never profitable, even after Dad moved it further downtown, so after a couple of years, he had to give it up and look elsewhere for ways to make money.

Although Ronnie disappeared from my life for almost half a century, I still thought about him sometimes—especially whenever I drove through East St. Louis. I wondered where he was and what he was doing. And every birthday for the next couple of decades I thought about the child we might have had, wondering if it had been a boy or girl and calculating, each birthday, how old it would be if it had lived.

But life goes on, and even in the midst of all our struggles, we continued to participate in things unrelated to the chaos at church. Although my yearbook indicates a notable lack of extracurricular activities during my sophomore year of high school, my grades remained high. Sometime in my junior year, I won an audition to sing "St. Louis Blues" on a teen talent show on KMOX radio in St. Louis called "Teen O'Clock Time," and that spring I sang another song for the popular "Junior Jam" at Belleville High School, for which my mother accompanied me on the piano. I even started a new romance during my senior year with a boy who was a couple of years older than I. He was delightful and fun loving, and we stayed together for a couple of years, getting engaged during Christmas break of my freshman year of college. But marriage for us was not to be, because in the summer of 1957, while working in Dad's used bookstore between my freshman and sophomore years, I met the man who would become my husband and the father of my children.

I wasn't going back to Oklahoma State in the fall, since Dad had told me if I didn't want to major in architecture, I could just come home and go to the community college. He was really disappointed that I had chosen to major in English, even though books were the love of his life. He wanted me to be a doctor, or lawyer, or architect. Why did anyone need to go to college to read books? In fact, I suspect he thought that my professors might have too much influence on my opinions of what I read. Dad had excellent taste in literature, but he never let the critics' opinion influence him. "I don't care what anyone says about a book," he told me once, "if it doesn't hold my interest in the first fifty pages, I put it down and move on." But when a fellow book-lover came into my life, I think he forgot about his ambitions for me in his joy at finding someone who might prove to be an ally in the family.

Harold Piety, having recently arrived in East St. Louis to work as a sportswriter for the *East St. Louis Journal* (later named the *Metro-East Journal*), was staying in a boarding house just a few blocks from the bookstore, which he had to pass every day on his way home. One day he could no longer resist the siren lure of books and stopped in to look around. As customers were rare, it was inevitable that we would begin to talk. He ended up staying for four hours.

"What does that ring mean?" he asked when he saw the diamond on my left ring finger.

"It means I'm engaged."

"When are you getting married?"

When I said I didn't know, he announced with finality, "If you don't know when you're getting married, you have no business being engaged."

The white shirt he was wearing under his sports coat looked as if it had just come out of the box, and with his dark hair, hazel eyes and olive skin, he was strikingly handsome. Unlike Dad and Ronnie, he was rather short—about my height, which was 5'7"—but his barrel chest and confident manner gave him a larger presence. I couldn't help noticing, though, that his fingernails were bitten to the quick. After looking around awhile, he asked me to hold a biography of *Xenophon* for him until his payday the following Tuesday. I'm not sure he ever read it, but I was impressed with his selection. I suspect that was the idea. And it gave him an excuse to come back soon.

For the next couple of weeks, he drove me to my classes at the junior college when I finished working in the bookstore, and my fiancé, unaware of what was going on, picked me up after school. Finally, unable to continue with the deceit, I broke off my engagement. My fiancé was a very nice young man who seemed to love me very much, and I genuinely cared for him. But he was no competition for the glamorous older man. "Your press agent," my fiancé sneered during the unhappy days of our breakup. One evening after class, when Harold picked me up, my former fiancé almost ran us off the road. Luckily for him—and for us—his better judgment prevailed, and we all escaped unscathed.

While my fiancé had been a fun-loving, gregarious young man, this new man in my life was clearly a loner and a bit pompous. A few weeks into the first semester that fall, we were sitting in the bookstore when I told him I had given myself an IQ test in my psychology class. I told him my score, adding "but I don't know if that's right, because I gave the test to myself."

That was higher than his score, he said, which had been tested in the Navy.

"Then my score can't be right!" I responded. "I'm sure your IQ is higher than mine."

"Oh, I don't doubt that your IQ is higher, but I know I'm a hell of a lot smarter than you are," he declared smugly.

In those days, most girls dreamed of finding a husband who was older, taller, stronger, smarter, and richer than she, so I guess I should have been glad that he was so smart and confident, but his remark did sting a little, even though I was pretty sure that he *was* smarter than I was.

For years I thought that when I fell in love with Harold Piety, I was still looking for my daddy. Like Dad, Harold loved books, and he was darkly handsome. And what I soon learned, to my delight, was that he and Dad shared a birthday: December 16, just 18 years apart. Several years later, Dad told me that when he saw the two of us together that first day, he had gone home and told Mom, "The boy Pat's going to marry is down in the bookstore."

In my eyes, Harold had a very colorful history. Not only was he a sportswriter, a career which sounded glamorous to the 18-year-old me, but he had also served in the U.S. Navy and traveled abroad. Ever since I had read *Around the World in 11 Years*, when I was about 10 years old, I had longed to see the world, so I was fascinated by his tales of the time he spent in Cuba and in France even if it was mostly in bars and dives, doing what sailors are said to do in foreign ports.

Having lost his mother to tuberculosis at an early age, Harold had spent most of his childhood, along with his four siblings, in an orphanage in Little Rock. His father, who was chairman of the Communist Party in Arkansas during the 1930s and '40s, was the object of FBI surveillance. Through his contacts, he heard that the Little Rock draft board was planning to draft him into World War II to get him out of the country, even though he had served in World War I, had a wife in a TB sanitarium, and five pre-school children. So he headed them off by enlisting in the army, where he quickly became an officer in charge of commanding some French troops. After the war, he married a refugee from a Communist country and remained in Europe until the mid-1950s as a director for the International Red Cross. There was more exotic stuff in Harold's family history, and I found it all incredibly romantic. And, touched by his tales of life in the orphanage (which he always referred to as "the home"), I wanted to give him a home and family. Like Desdemona with Othello, "I loved him for the dangers he had passed."

What clinched the deal, though, was the fact that my whole family loved him. Dad adored him and even my mother took a liking to him right away, which was shocking, since he smoked cigarettes and was not a churchgoer. What's more, he liked her, something my previous boyfriends had not done. For my little brother, Harold filled in the gaps left by Dad, who had no interest in sports or a lot of other things boys John's age liked, so John and Harold bonded immediately. Clearly, Harold was meant to be a member of the family. In fact, somewhere in this world there may still be a photo of the two of us, taken during those early days, in which, our arms around each other, our rather large noses glinting in the sunlight, we look almost like twins. Throughout our lives together—and, indeed, to this day—I have always thought of him as a member of my family.

One night a month or so after we met, when we were having dinner together, I confided, "I don't know if I'm in love with you, but I sure would like to marry you!"

"I feel the same way about you," he said.

I wanted to get married as soon as possible, and I think Harold was eager to start making babies. He said he would like to have at least six, like his dad, who had fathered another son in his second marriage. "A man should choose a mate the same way he chooses a good horse for breeding," Harold wrote to his dad. "She should have high intelligence, good health, and a wide pelvis for childbearing." I'm paraphrasing here because I don't have a copy of that letter, but I do remember that Harold's dad, who wasn't known for his own sensitivity to women's issues, was rather shocked by Harold's unapologetic rationale for marrying me. "Son, that's not a very romantic way to talk about your bride-to-be," he wrote back.

In spite of his rather cold-eyed formula for choosing a mate, Harold *did* have a romantic side. He wooed me by singing "Green Eyes" and the love song from *Tales of Hoffmann* as we rode around town in his spiffy new VW bug, and he brought his portable record player to the bookstore to play Wagner's *Tristan and Isolde* for me, which, he explained, was very erotic. We spent many afternoons in the bookstore reading the raciest parts of Balzac and D. H. Lawrence to each other, but during our courtship, he never said "I love you" or "You're beautiful." Instead, he told me, "You're very attractive," and "I'm fond of you." I couldn't very well complain, considering the frank nature of my proposal to him, but his reticence did bother me a bit, because I was beginning to feel pretty romantic about him.

Wanting to give us more time to consider our decision—and hoping to save up a little money for the wedding—Mom tried to get me to put off the nuptials at least until the end of the academic year, but I wouldn't hear of it.

"Pat, why don't you do what your mother wants and wait until summer?" my Sunday school teacher asked one morning in class.

"I'm getting married to give this baby a name!" I shot back. *That ought to shut everybody up*, I thought. (Have I mentioned that I could have a smart mouth at times?) In truth, I probably feared that I *would* get pregnant again, as Harold and I had become intimate no more than a month after we met, and I desperately didn't want to go through anything like what had happened to me a couple of years earlier. During sex I was always haunted by anxiety about getting caught, and I couldn't wait to be able make love without worrying about somebody beating down the door. It seemed so amazing to me that a religious ceremony and a legal document could make something that had been such a terrible sin suddenly just fine.

Besides, I wanted to get out of my mother's house.

So on January 25, 1958, five months after our first meeting and three months after my 19th birthday, Harold and I were married in the church that had been the scene of all our family's troubles. I had wanted to be married at home, or, failing that, in the Methodist Church across the street from our house because it was prettier and had an organ, but Mom insisted on going back to Bethel Tabernacle. She arranged to rent an electric organ for the occasion, and Uncle Bill sang "Bless This House" (my choice) and "Sheep May Safely Graze" (Harold's choice), accompanied by Uncle Bill's friend, Bill Hart. His voice shaking, Dad performed the ceremony. When he asked, "Who giveth this woman . . . ?" my mother responded, "I do." But, like my mother before me, I had made sure that the word "obey" was deleted from the ceremony. Neither Mom nor I had ever cottoned to the idea of blind obedience, especially to a man.

There is no way to tell the whole story of my 20-year marriage to Harold Piety. Just as I spent a lot of the first part of my life in wistful nostalgia for those early years on the road and in Waxahachie, I have devoted a significant portion of the years since my divorce to aching longing for that period in which, together, we built the family of our dreams. Of course, everything wasn't perfect—life never is, except in brief moments. But I still remember those years when we were raising a family together as some of the best of my adult life.

In a little over four years of marriage, Harold and I became parents of three beautiful baby girls. The first came nine months and three weeks after our wedding night (were those church ladies counting on their fingers?), the second 17 months later, and the third just 25 months after that. So my transition from college student to mother of three was disconcertingly rapid. While I had always thought of myself as older than my peers, it was only after the girls were born that I began to realize how young I really was.

Still wracked with guilt over all the trouble I had caused my family, and not convinced that I deserved to be happy, I anticipated disaster at every turn. During the first pregnancy, I worried that I wouldn't be able to love my baby as much as I loved my brother, and when the second baby was on the way, I feared that I wouldn't love her as much as the first. By the time the third arrived, I was more confident that my love could expand to embrace any number of children, but I couldn't escape the anxious foreboding of catastrophe, and my nerves were constantly on edge from trying to keep them all well and safe. Before long, I found myself in a cycle of tranquilizers to calm me down and pep pills to keep me awake. What I had, one doctor told me, was the "Housewife's Syndrome."

During those years when the babies were small, there were times when I was too tired for sex. It was the late 1950s and early 1960s, when women's magazines like the *Ladies Home Journal* carried articles about the problem of female frigidity, and when I was unresponsive to Harold's advances, he suggested that maybe I didn't really like sex, or maybe I found it more exciting outside of marriage. The implied accusation that I could be frigid was very disturbing to me. One thing on which I had always prided myself was my sexual attractiveness and my ability as a lover. My self-confidence was shaken.

To make matters worse, I was gradually realizing that Harold, despite sharing a birthday and a love of books with my dad, was more like my mother in ways that I found hard to take. He had strong ideas about The One Right Way to do things, and he couldn't help sharing his opinion when I deviated from what he deemed the correct course. He knew exactly how many of his chocolate chip cookies would fit on the cookie sheet, and he believed the only correct way to make mashed potatoes was to put the them through a ricer and warm the milk before adding it. His potatoes were light and fluffy, while mine sometimes had lumps; once when we sat down to dinner, one of the girls asked, "Are these Mommy potatoes or Daddy potatoes?" Another time, sensing that I wasn't fully living up to the role of mother as he envisioned it, I asked him where he thought I fell short. "You don't bake cookies with the girls," he said.

"But you do that!" I pointed out. What I should have added was, "I take them for rides in the country and read to them and make up silly songs for them and march around the house with them to band music, and chauffeur them to lessons of all kinds, and buy them formals at the Goodwill so they can play dress-up, and water colors so they can paint." But I couldn't help feeling that I didn't measure up.

Harold's concern with correctness and propriety had almost certainly been instilled in him during adolescence when a wealthy aunt had rescued him and his siblings from the orphanage and undertaken to refine their manners from what she apparently considered their hillbilly upbringing in Arkansas. Nevertheless, I saw his efforts to educate me as further proof of my inadequacy. This "poor little orphan boy" for whom I had wanted to create a home and family had, through hard experience, acquired a degree of self-sufficiency that often left me feeling I had little to contribute to our partnership beyond making babies, taking care of them, and cleaning house.

To complicate matters, Harold had a degree of emotional insularity—very likely a result of his being separated from his mother at the age of three—that was incompatible with my touchy-feely, let's-talk-about-it nature. I longed for demonstrations of affection and was tormented by fears that he didn't love me when they weren't forthcoming.

Still, he was a doting and helpful father, he was a reliable provider, and he was uncomplaining when I decided to return to college part-time to pursue my education after the birth of our second child. But he was older, had a more retentive memory, a larger vocabulary and more experience, and he frequently reminded me of all this in not-so-subtle ways. While I admired him for his intelligence, knowledge and writing skill, I bridled at his every criticism and his attempts to instruct me.

I should have seen it coming: Once, while we were still getting acquainted during his visits to the bookstore, he had criticized the way I swept the floor. Grabbing the broom, he showed me the proper way to do it. "Proper" was a frequent word in his vocabulary. His criticism reminded me of my mother's insistence that "the dishes aren't done until the floor is swept!" or her contention that I twisted clothes in the wrong direction when I was helping with the wash. I was more like my dad, who had batted cross-handed in the softball games we played at church picnics.

In the first couple of months after our marriage, Harold and I had continued the practice of reading to each other that we had started during our courtship in the bookstore. Unlike Harold, I tend to forget most books I have read or movies I have seen almost immediately unless they have made a very strong impression on me, but I still have fond memories of specific passages from Peter Freuchen's *My Life in the Frozen North*, which we read together in bed during the first few weeks of our marriage. A few months later, however, after we had moved to the efficiency apartment in my parents' basement and he was taking a course in linguistics at Washington University, he cut me short when I tried to share a moving passage from *The Trojan Women* quoted in a book by my favorite professor at Oklahoma State. "I'm not interested in undergraduate textbooks," he informed me. There are lots of jokes about wives who never forget past slights. I guess I'm one of them, because I still feel the sting of that rebuff more than half a century later.

A few years later, while I was attending classes at Southern Illinois-Edwardsville, to complete the requirements for my bachelor's degree, Harold volunteered to write a feature story about one of my professors. This professor, who had founded a new academic journal for the Midwest Modern Language Association, was a rather snobbish academic, very taken with Henry James. Although I didn't share my professor's appreciation of James (I found James's sentences incredibly prolix), I had made A's in both of the courses I took from him. When I told him Harold wanted to write a feature story about him for the paper, he was very excited and graciously invited us to his office, where he showed us his first editions and fine prints on the office walls. "Be sure to save several copies of the article for me!" he said. But when I opened the paper the day the story came out, my stomach did a swan dive. "Symbiosis is a wonderful thing," it began. It went on to explain that, under the "publish or perish" imperative at institutions of higher learning, professors were compelled to get their work published if they wanted to hold onto their jobs and advance their careers, but since most of them were such poor writers, they couldn't sell their writing commercially. So, the article concluded, they had to create academic journals for that purpose. Harold had even gone to the trouble to verify that this particular professor had never had an article accepted by the parent MLA journal, the Mecca for English professors. After the article came out, my professor never spoke to me again, and when I passed him on campus, he would turn his head.

So there were some undercurrents of discord between us almost from the very beginning. During the early years of our marriage, although we tried to hide our differences from our children, there were many nights when I lay in bed quietly sobbing until 2 a.m. or later, feeling guilty about keeping Harold awake when he had to get up early to go to work. Today, if you asked me what I was so unhappy about on one of those nights, I wouldn't be able to give a specific answer. Maybe, like my mother after the birth of my brother, I was suffering from postpartum depression. Or maybe I was just trying to handle too much change at once.

After a while, I began to notice that I was more critical of Harold than usual whenever my parents were around. They liked him so much that I guess I was trying to suggest to them that he wasn't perfect. But if that was my intention, it backfired badly. Once, when Dad had dropped by to see us, he was sitting at the kitchen table with us when I began complaining about something Harold had done—or not done. "Honey, be careful, or you'll end up being like your mom," Dad warned. I never told either Dad or Harold that I went straight to the bathroom and sat in a tub of hot water, razor blade on the edge of the tub, as I contemplated slitting my wrists. For years, I thought nothing in the world could be worse than to be like my mom.

Despite these problems, though, there were many more good times than bad in our marriage. If I skip over them too lightly, it is because recalling them is so incredibly poignant. For this book I made a list of pleasant memories from those days—a list so long that I knew I could never share it all. There were the camping trips, the road trips to California and Hilton Head, and the train rides to Chicago and D.C. to visit Harold's brothers. At home in Ohio, where we moved after my 30th birthday, there were concerts, plays, ballets and art exhibits in which our daughters showed off their considerable talents. But many of the best times were the kinds of things that happen in families on a regular basis—Scrabble games, family movie nights, going out for pizza—little things that seem unremarkable at the time, but which result in some of the most treasured memories of a lifetime.

There were some special moments, too, when Harold and I were alone together. I remember lying beside him with my arms wrapped around his sleeping form, telling myself, "I don't want to live without him. When he dies, I want to die, too." After lovemaking, sometimes I would tiptoe into my babies' bedrooms and kiss their sleeping forms, thankful for these tangible gifts of our love. After the disaster of my teens, I had never thought I could be so lucky. And even when things weren't going well, the very idea of separating my children from their father was unbearable. I loved them more than life itself, I knew how much they loved their father and he them, and I wanted them all to be happy.

But more than once I woke up with an aching in my gut, sobbing from a nightmare in which I had dreamed that Harold didn't love me. He told me one time that my need for love was a hole too deep for him to fill, and perhaps he was right. I wasn't sure that I was lovable.

During the late 1960s, Harold was beginning to fight with his editor over how to report on the racial tensions that would eventually tear East St. Louis apart, reducing that once All-American City to the half-deserted, battle-scarred town it still is today. After graduating from sportswriter to religion editor (in which position he got a kick out of answering the phone with "Piety, Religion"), he had moved on to reporting on local civil rights activities. In the meantime, I had begun teaching third grade at Central School in O'Fallon, Illinois, on a limited provisional certificate, which allowed me to teach without a degree, so long as I continued to accrue a certain number of credit hours every two years. During the summers, I attended classes at the emerging Southern Illinois University-Edwardsville campus. At the same time, in addition to reporting on civil rights, Harold was producing a twice-weekly column called "Humble Pie," in which he often wrote about our family life. "That sounds just like you, Pat," one of my classmates joked about a column in which Harold pictured me as a sarcastic, critical wife. The other students in my little circle of friends laughed good-naturedly, but I remember feeling a bit embarrassed and defensive.

Harold was a prolific writer. Often when he came home from work, he would spread out the paper on the kitchen table, thumping his index finger on story after story, saying, "I wrote that, and that, and that . . ." Through his column, he had also achieved a certain level of local fame. So it was a terrible blow to his ego when he was banished from the newspaper's main office in East St. Louis to the back room of a Hallmark greeting card store in Collinsville to write obituaries. "You need to learn how to write all over again," his boss had told him.

The problem was that Harold had had the temerity to go out into the community and interview witnesses during the growing racial unrest in East St. Louis in the mid-1960s and, unfortunately for him, the facts he discovered sometimes conflicted with the police reports. This did not make the paper's publishers happy. Once, when he wrote about an angry outbreak by black teenagers after fire officials had broken up their party for overcrowding, he came back from lunch to find that another reporter was rewriting his story to make it more incendiary. "Bands of angry black youths roamed the streets of East St. Louis, vandalizing local businesses and terrorizing bypassing motorists . . ." is how I remember the opening line of the rewritten story.

Another time, the police report said that a local civil rights demonstrator had been injured by a Molotov cocktail, but witnesses told Harold the man had been fired on by a sheriff's deputy from a passing car. Sure enough, when Harold interviewed the attending physician, he found that the man's injury had contained buckshot, and he reported this fact in his story. A member of the American Newspaper Guild, Harold couldn't easily be fired, but the paper had the power to make his life miserable. His banishment to the Hallmark store was designed to do just that.

A strong believer in equal rights since childhood, I was proud of Harold's courage in reporting the truth—and very angry about the way he was treated by his editor. Together, we had some interesting interactions with some of the local leaders of civil rights activities, both black and white, attending public demonstrations and forming several long-term friendships among African Americans in East St. Louis. Once, we even invited some black revolutionaries to a cookout at our home in O'Fallon. I've always been amused to imagine how our neighbors in that all-white little town of 4,000 must have felt when they saw those dashiki-clad young black men with their Afro hairdos standing around the barbecue grill in our back yard.

Back then, the nearby town of Belleville, where I had graduated from high school, was mainly populated by middle- and upper-middle-class whites, many of German descent. A small group of African Americans lived there—in fact, our high school was already integrated when I entered it in 1952—but, for the most part, the blacks lived in neighboring East St. Louis. Many East St. Louis residents worked at the stockyards, the railroad yards, at nearby Monsanto or loading barges on the Mississippi. So it was more of a blue-collar town than Belleville, but a thriving one.

During that period when Harold was reporting on civil rights, someone from the Anti-Defamation League called to tell him that a cover organization for the John Birch Society called TRAIN (To Restore American Independence Now) was attracting large crowds to evening meetings in the public schools in Belleville. Since Harold was unable to attend the next scheduled meeting, I decided to go and see for myself what was happening.

Some 200 people were gathered at this meeting, at which the speaker showed a movie purporting to illustrate how the Communists, "parading behind legitimate grievances," had infiltrated and overthrown governments like those in Cuba and Algeria. I couldn't help noticing that whenever a quotation from Communist Leon Trotsky flashed on the screen, the voiceover sounded exactly like that of Vice President Hubert Humphrey, a not-so-subtle attempt at subliminal persuasion. After the movie, when the floor was opened for discussion, I put on my best "dumb female" face and rose to ask a question:

"Uh, yes," I started hesitantly, "I noticed that the movie kept saying the Communists take over countries by parading behind legitimate grievances. . ." When the leader nodded in agreement, I continued, "and I was just wondering how we, here in America, could get rid of these legitimate grievances so that the Communists wouldn't have anything to hide behind."

Clearly, that wasn't the question the leader had hoped for. When he started to explain that, in fact, Americans didn't have any legitimate grievances, I gestured toward the lone African American man who had mustered up the courage to attend this racist propaganda meeting:

"This young man and his wife" I said, "have been trying to rent a house in Belleville for months. When they call, they are told that the property is available, but after they arrive, the landlords keep telling them it has already been rented."

Although I didn't know the young man I had just put in the Birch Society crosshairs, I had heard about his problem and had spoken to him briefly before the meeting that night. I thought later that I should have asked his permission to use him as an example, since I could have gotten him in real trouble, but, as has happened to me too many times in my life, I didn't realize what I was going to say until the words were out of my mouth. Luckily, though, the more vocal members of the crowd chose to focus their outrage on me.

"The Communists send people like you to these meetings to get people stirred up and confused!" one man yelled, pointing his finger at me. "I've seen you here before!"

It wasn't true, of course. This was my first meeting at TRAIN—and my last, although I had gone with my mother to a small meeting of the John Birch Society in one of her friends' home, just to see what the enemy was up to. But I had kept my mouth shut there, knowing Mom would not have it otherwise. She always thought it was impolite to disagree with people out loud.

So the problems between Harold and me were not rooted in our political or social beliefs. The problem for me was that he didn't talk about his feelings, so I didn't really know him. I thought of him as much more mature and well balanced than I, and, in retrospect, I realize that I often related to him as a child to a parent. I told him everything and expected him to be understanding and detached. Once when I asked him to consider going to marriage counseling, he refused. "I think I have achieved a delicate balance in my mental health and I don't want to do anything to upset it," he explained. But I craved more emotional intimacy.

So I had an affair with a classmate. "Affair" is actually too formal a word for the couple of times that I sneaked away for an hour or two with this young man. And the sad irony is that I never once thought I was in love with him or doubted my love for Harold. I explained this to Harold when I compounded my sins by confessing what I had done, but my foolish venture into infidelity damaged our relationship in ways that never fully healed. "If I ever have an affair," he warned me, "you won't know about it."

Nevertheless, when I graduated from Southern Illinois University at Edwardsville in the spring of 1967, there were tears of pride in Harold's eyes, and Dad was there beside him, beaming. Mom, however, was on a Caribbean cruise with her sister, Edith.

By the summer of 1968, Harold had left the Metro-East Journal to become press secretary for Illinois Rep. Paul Simon, who was running for lieutenant governor. It was a year that stands out in my life—and in the lives of many others, I'm sure. There were demonstrations everywhere against the war in Vietnam, against racism, against poverty. Political tensions were high. While working with the campaign, Harold happened to be in the streets of Chicago during the famous demonstration over the Democratic Convention. Not an official part of the crowd, he was nevertheless in sympathy with their cause, and he told me all about it. When the police tried to clear the streets of the demonstrators, he said, comedian and activist Dick Gregory explained that they were all his friends, and they were not unlawfully congregating—they were just going down the street to his house.

Back home in O'Fallon, Illinois, I was taking care of the children and commuting to Washington University in St. Louis, where I was carrying a full load in the graduate school. Every Monday, I would drive Harold across the Mississippi to the airport or the train station and, from there, I would go on to my classes. A babysitter would stay with the children after school until I got home. After dropping Harold off, I frequently had attacks of diarrhea caused by my extreme anxiety that he might be killed in a plane crash during the week and never return. As it was my first semester of graduate school on scholarship at a highly regarded university, I was also feeling stressed about my performance.

One Monday when I dropped Harold off at Union Station, I returned to my car to find that it was leaking some kind of fluid, so I had to find a repair shop in St. Louis and take the bus on to my classes. Somehow I found a shop that would allow me to pick up the car up after I got out of class, which would be well past their closing time. When my class ended, the sky was growing dark and a faint drizzle was falling. Being unfamiliar with St. Louis bus routes, I wound up standing on the wrong corner for an hour or more. It was October 7, 1968, my 30th birthday. Exactly half of my life had passed since that fateful 15th birthday, but I had struggled with melancholy on every Oct. 7 since, so as I stood on that corner in the chilly evening drizzle waiting for a bus that never came, I was overcome with loneliness and depression.

Eventually, I found the right corner, rode the bus to the repair shop to pick up my car, and drove back across the river to Illinois, where I discovered that the babysitter and my three little girls had baked a birthday cake for me and filled the house with balloons and homemade cards. For several hours before I arrived, the babysitter said, they had rushed to the window each time they heard a car outside, only to be disappointed that it wasn't mine. When I finally walked in the door and found their sweet welcome, I was so exhausted and moved that I burst into tears.

Many years later, as my daughter Julia and I were driving through St. Louis, I pointed out the corner on which I had stood so miserably, recalling how wonderful it had been to find that she and her sisters had prepared a surprise party for me when I got home. But her response took me totally off guard: "What I remember about that night was that you cried, and I thought we had done something wrong." When I heard that, I was struck by how children can misinterpret what is going on in the world around them. In fact, we don't have to be children to see things from a very different perspective than others might do. So as I tell my story, I am well aware that others may see the events in a different light.

While I was attending grad school in St. Louis, I couldn't help being a little envious that Harold was in the middle of all the action in Chicago and around the state. But, to be fair, there was plenty of action in St. Louis, as well. As I waded through downtown traffic during the 1968 World Series games on my way to class, demonstrators were questioning how Americans could be idling away their time and spending money on a sports event when there were still so many hungry and jobless people right there in St. Louis and young men were dying on the battlefield in Vietnam. On campus, the Students for a Democratic Society were doing everything in their power to draw attention away from ivory tower academics to more immediate, pressing social problems. (The following spring, Wash U students would burn down the campus Air Force ROTC building a few hours after the May 4, 1970, Kent State incident, where National Guard soldiers shot and killed four student demonstrators.)

Yielding to pressure from students, Washington University officials had even instituted some changes of their own. When I entered school that fall, I was informed that the graduate school, well known for its academic rigor, would no longer give grades to students but would simply record a "pass" or "fail" for each course completed. Although the reading and writing assignments continued to be heavy (I was assigned 27 novels to read in one course and 14 in another), the classes often veered off into political subjects. In one class, we were treated to a visit from the Catonsville Nine, a group of Catholic activists who, on May 17, 1968, had gone to the draft board in Catonsville, Maryland, taken 378 draft files to the parking lot, poured home-made napalm over them, and set them on fire. As part of the campus lecture series, David Halberstam, *New York Times* reporter and winner of the 1964 Pulitzer Prize for international reporting, came to talk to us about his experiences in Vietnam and his earlier travels with Martin Luther King, Jr. I was thrilled to be a part of this exciting intellectual and social activity, but I already knew that, for me, the party would soon be over.

I had been awarded a full-tuition scholarship to Wash U the previous spring—a dream come true—and under the terms of the scholarship, I could continue straight through to a doctorate, so long as I kept my grades up. When I received the letter, I was exhilarated and full of hope. But over the summer, before I even had a chance to enter school, Harold had become disenchanted with Illinois politics and began looking around for another job. He was disgusted by the spectacle of Simon, the fabled Boy Scout of Illinois, having to cozy up in public to politicians of questionable character like Secretary of State Paul Powell. (After Powell's death, it was discovered that although he had never earned more than $30,000 a year, he left an estate worth more than $4 million.) So, after the November 1968 election (which Democrat Simon won, while the governorship went to Republican Sam Shapiro), Harold moved to Ohio to accept a position with the *Dayton Journal Herald*, leaving me to care for the girls and try to sell the house in O'Fallon while commuting to graduate school across the river in St. Louis.

Harold was the family breadwinner, and the family had to go where the jobs were. Case closed. So after one semester, I gave up my scholarship, managed to sell the house (despite the leaky basement), and moved the girls and myself to Dayton to join Harold. But to this day, when I pass the Washington University campus, I feel a pang of regret that I can't go back in time and achieve my youthful dream of a Ph.D. from that highly regarded institution.

The first year in Dayton, in 1969, was the start of an exciting new life for our family. Harold enjoyed his job, we had no money problems, I was temporarily neither working nor going to school, we were getting along well, and the girls seemed to be adjusting well to their new school. Everybody was happy. For the first eight months, we lived in a large, old rented house with a small wooded area in back, where we liked to play on a rope swing that hung from one of the trees. In the big, grassy vacant lot next door, sometimes we played Whiffle Ball.

With a friend whose husband had worked with mine in East St. Louis and who was now his colleague at the *Dayton Journal Herald*, I joined a women's bowling league. After league play finished in the morning, I would catch a ride with her to the Big Boy restaurant near the girls' school to treat them to lunch. In first, third, and fifth grade at the time of our move, they would walk together from the school to the restaurant and wait for me to show up and join them. After lunch, I would walk with them back to school and then on to our rented house a few blocks away. One day when my ride was late, my heart melted when I arrived to see them sitting at a booth with anxious little faces, wondering how they were going to pay for the lunches they had just eaten. I loved them so much.

That year, I also volunteered as a Pink Lady at nearby Good Samaritan Hospital. And on mornings when I didn't have any other responsibilities, I would take Harold to work and then drive for hours through the city and out on back-country roads, exploring our new home state. I loved wandering around the countryside, finding my way home guided only by the sun.

And, of course, I was always reading. But I wasn't yet ready to give up on my dream of obtaining a Ph.D. in English. So by the fall of 1969, I transferred my twelve graduate hours of "pass" from Wash U to the University of Dayton, where I received a graduate assistantship to teach freshman composition while working toward a master's degree. At the time, the nearest institutions that offered Ph.D.'s in English were Miami University, in Miami, Ohio, and Ohio State, in Columbus, neither of which was in very comfortable commuting distance, so I didn't know if I would continue past a master's degree. But in December 1970 I received my master's degree and went on to teach college composition the following fall at Wright State University.

Eight months after our arrival in Dayton, Harold and I bought a two-and-a-half-story house in a lovely old integrated city neighborhood called Dayton View. It had big, terraced back yard where Harold delighted in growing strawberries, raspberries, sour cherries, and apples, from which he made pies and jams and jellies each year to spread on his delicious homemade bread. He wasn't as dedicated to lawn mowing, though, a task that often fell to me. I was definitely the one more concerned with the physical appearance of our home and yard, while he was the more domestic one, and sometimes we were able to work out win/win compromises. He was a relatively early riser and I liked to sleep late, and since he enjoyed cooking, for a couple of years he got up first and fixed a huge breakfast for the girls—biscuits and gravy, pancakes, eggs benedict, something different every day—while I remained in bed. After the girls went off to school, he would crawl back in bed with me to have sex. So everybody was happy—until the girls informed him that they were getting fat and didn't want to eat such big breakfasts anymore. He was visibly depressed for a while after being informed that they no longer needed him for this morning ritual.

In the Dayton View neighborhood we became part of a diverse group of neighbors who enjoyed frequent block parties, visits in one another's homes, and outings to concerts at the Dayton Art Institute or the Dayton Philharmonic. Shortly after Harold's arrival, he had been promoted from feature writer to editorial writer, a job uniquely suited to his talents and abilities, since he was well versed in history and international affairs and possessed a steel-trap memory for facts and dates. Through his job, we met fascinating people from both the local community and other parts of the world.

After Harold started doing research on the Middle East, we often attended events hosted by Arab Americans and Palestinians and we reciprocated with dinner parties for them in our home. In our neighborhood there were three Jewish houses of worship—Reform, Conservative, and Orthodox—as well as a Jewish school, so during the same week, we might enjoy an evening of coffee and lively conversation with several of our Jewish neighbors. We also met a number of interesting people through my job at Wilberforce University, where I was teaching by then, and through Tamara's first boyfriend, a young man from Iran who was studying engineering at the University of Dayton. During one memorable week, we hosted a party for Mohammad and his friends, complete with Persian food and music. The next night, we held a party for my African students from Wilberforce. The following day, one of the children from down the block made me smile when he asked, "What kind of people are you going to have over tonight?"

During this period, we sometimes hosted informal evening Friends meetings with Quakers we had met through the American Friends Service Committee, a regional office of which was a few blocks from our home, and, on invitation from one of Harold's friends who was an attorney, we began attending services at the nearby Church of the Brethren. For a precious few years, our life in Dayton View was almost a Utopia of diversity and harmony. Things were a lot tougher on the girls, though.

Although the racial balance of Dayton View was almost 50/50 in 1969, the student population in the public schools was approximately 90 percent black, a fact of which we were unaware when we had decided to more there. Several of our neighbors were older, with no children living at home, and many of our white neighbors who still had children at home sent them to Catholic schools, the Jewish school a couple of blocks away, or a private school in the suburbs. So attending schools in which they were a tiny minority in the racially troubled 1970s was not easy for our girls. They experienced a good deal of reverse racism from some of their classmates and were often frightened by the more hostile ones. "I would never do that to my children," my mother said. But I was a fanatic about integration. I had read so much about the evils of segregation, and I had been so moved by the pictures of little black children in the South braving a gauntlet of angry whites to exercise their right to go to integrated schools, that I thought I could do no less than the courageous mothers of those black children by offering up my children to the cause of integrated schools.

Still, I worried about the girls a lot and tried to help them through as best I could, quizzing them daily about what was going on at school and often picking them up after school or having a friend do it when I had to work. They still bear some scars from those experiences, but they had a few outstanding, dedicated teachers and they formed some friendships with black classmates. They also gained an understanding of racism that many white children in America have not had the opportunity to acquire. I am extremely proud to say that, as adults, they are all strong advocates of equal rights.

There was also a higher crime rate in our inner city neighborhood than in the suburbs, which created a certain level of tension and watchfulness, but despite the problems, I think we all got considerable pleasure from those first few years at the house in Dayton View. The girls were taking lessons of all kinds, from ballet to gymnastics to violin, figure skating, and guitar, and all three of them were accepted into the very progressive Living Arts program offered by the Dayton Public Schools—Tamara in creative writing, Marilyn ("Titi") in art, and Julia in performing arts, where she performed alongside the young Rob Lowe, who would go on to a career in movies and TV. We all loved our house, with its front porch swing, living room fireplace, huge attic room, and gently terraced back yard. Harold and I were having some good times as a couple, too. Shortly after our divorce, he wrote to me that our first ten years in Dayton had been the best of his life.

The trouble stared when he began writing editorials about the Middle East.

A few months after Harold was promoted to the editorial staff, the paper ceased publishing temporarily when the Newspaper Guild went on strike. As a member of management, Harold was not on strike, so he decided to spend his time doing research on the Middle East. When he began his research, his views were largely reflective of those of most Americans: that Israel was a brave little democracy surrounded by enemies determined to drive it into the sea. As he read book after history book, talked to experts on the issues, and perused some of the U.N. documents relating to the 1967 war, he began to change his mind. The paper even sponsored a trip for him to the Middle East, where he interviewed prominent Israelis and residents of a kibbutz as well as representatives of the Palestine Liberation Organization. When he began writing editorials that there would be no peace in the Middle East until Palestinians had their own independent state, the shit hit the fan.

Before long, a delegation of supporters of Israel visited the paper's editorial board, demanding that Harold stop writing about the Middle East. Since this group contained the owners of the largest grocery store chain in the area, on which the paper relied for a good deal of its revenue, the editors paid attention. They told Harold to tone down his editorials. Despite the fact that he was a knowledgeable and gifted writer, Harold's fatal weakness was a lack of diplomacy. In his mind, if he presented what he considered to be the facts in a logical way, readers should be able to consider his argument without becoming emotional. This was the second attempt by a newspaper to muzzle him on issues he thought important, and this time he became so angry that he sometimes took to shouting and cursing in editorial meetings. Once, in an effort to help his colleagues see things from another perspective, he brought in the anti-Zionist Jewish activist, Ned Hanauer, to talk with the editorial board. Hanauer, founder of an organization called "Search for Justice and Equality in Palestine," held views that were at least as "radical" as Harold's—and probably more so. But after the meeting, Harold's boss said to him, "Why can't you be more reasonable, like Ned?" Despite the fact that diplomacy wasn't his long suit, however, Harold had become known as something of an expert on the Middle East, both in Dayton and among people who were writing about the subject nationally, including the anti-Zionist Jewish scholar, Alfred M. Lilienthal. But the grocery store owners and others continued to put pressure on the paper and eventually, Harold's bosses told him that if he wanted to hold onto his job, he could no longer make public presentations on the subject, even on his own time. I will always be grateful to our Jewish friends in Dayton View who continued to be our friends even when they didn't agree with Harold's views on the Middle East. I know that some of them took a good deal of flack for doing so, and I respect them for their integrity.

It's not surprising, though, that Harold was becoming more difficult to live with at home during this time. Once, when he was raging to me about the situation at work, I begged him to try to calm down. "I'm afraid you might kill someone," I said, to which he responded, "I might!" There was never any danger, I hasten to add, that he was going to kill anyone. In the twenty years we were married, he never raised a hand to me or to anyone else, including the children, and we didn't own any firearms besides the shotgun I had bought for him years earlier to take on infrequent hunting trips. But he was very angry. His pride was hurt, he was worried about his job, and his frustration tolerance was at low ebb. At one point, he even contemplated quitting his job, without another one to go to. "The girls are in their teens," he said. "We will survive somehow." Fortunately, he didn't follow through on that impulse. While I was trying to cope with Harold's rage over his job, our girls were also going through some of the typical stages of teenagers and, being someone with a perpetually high anxiety level, I was often at a loss to know how to cope.

So I did what I had done before when things got too much for me to handle at home: I escaped into an affair. A year earlier, I had begun teaching at Wilberforce University in Xenia, about 30 miles away. I had really enjoyed my previous job, teaching at Wright State, but after three years there I resigned in frustration when I learned that no matter how good a teacher I might be, I would soon be out of a job because the university was opening a graduate program in English and had decided to replace all the non-Ph.D. instructors with graduate assistants. For a year after leaving Wright State, I was out of work, writing free book reviews for my husband's paper and taking any writing assignments I could find to build a portfolio. So when someone called to ask me if I would like to teach at Wilberforce University in Xenia, I jumped at the chance. At the time, I didn't even know that it was a Historically Black University, but that was certainly not a deterrent in my eyes. It was the 1970s, and at first I encountered a couple of students who were hostile to whites, but most of the students were exceptionally warm and welcoming, and the faculty was a delightful mix of races, nationalities and ethnicities. Although the job at Wilberforce didn't pay as much as my later positions, or even as much as the previous one at Wright State, it was the most enjoyable one of my life until after my retirement, when I started working on my "bucket list."

The Wilberforce colleague that I chose for my extramarital adventure was nine years my junior and, in my view, the epitome of exoticism. A West Indian, he had grown up in poverty and scrambled his way up the ladder to achieve a master's degree while sending money back to the islands to help his brother do the same. He was single and good-looking, he spoke with a delightful West Indian lilt, and he drove a second-hand but spotless Mercedes. After we became intimate, I learned that he was also secretly working on a Ph.D. at Northwestern University in Chicago—driving from Dayton to Chicago on Monday evenings so he could attend classes on all day Tuesday and then driving straight back to Dayton to show up in his office at Wilberforce on Wednesday. I was impressed by his energy and drive, and I found an element of intrigue in his secret trips to Chicago. True to form, I made the first move, and he responded with enthusiastic surprise.

I told my family that I had office hours on Thursday—which I did. But I my office hours were on Thursday afternoons, so I had a whole morning—three or four hours, almost every week—to spend with my young lover at his apartment in Xenia. I had always loved jazz, but at home our record collection consisted mainly of classical music, which Harold preferred. In my lover's apartment, the reel-to-reel recorder was always playing our favorites by groups like the Modern Jazz Quartet, Hubert Laws, and George Benson. Lying in bed, we traded stories of our childhoods, and later we both enjoyed drinking herbal tea at the table in his tiny kitchen. Because I was older and moved in the more sophisticated circles of Harold's acquaintances, I was probably as exotic in his eyes as he was in mine. Those mornings in his apartment were an escapist's paradise.

Although I was starting to fall in love with my West Indian, I never doubted that I still loved Harold. Since as far back as I could remember, I had been plagued by inclination to melodrama, in which the events of my life often seemed as dramatic and tragic as anything I read in the novels that had kept me enthralled most of my life, so I remember driving to work and back during that period with the song, "Torn Between Two Lovers" running on a loop in my head. Everything might have gone along smoothly, without a threat to my marriage and family, if I had not given in to the compulsion, eventually, to tell Harold about it. Was I simply trying to get my husband's attention or force him to make a decision for me?

I don't know. I don't know. I don't know.

All I know for sure is that it was terribly cruel mistake, with tragic consequences for me and everyone I loved.

Sometime after my revelation, Harold told me he had fallen in love with a young woman at work. He was 46 and she was 19, only a year older than our eldest daughter. She was a short, bouncy, brown-eyed blond with a wide, bright smile, as different from me as a female could be. I was devastated, but painfully aware that I had no moral grounds on which to object to my husband's transfer of affection.

For the next few months, we discussed our situation in secret, trying to keep the girls from knowing that the family they had always taken for granted was in grave danger of falling apart. I enrolled in a tennis class at the local community college, only to find out that Harold's new love was in the class, too. When I decided to drop out, she told Harold she was sorry I felt I had to withdraw because of her, and when he passed her message on to me, I re-enrolled, not wanting to let her believe that I had been intimidated by a girl who was literally half my age. I even took her to lunch once to find out what she was like. "I told Harold that if I met you, I would probably like you," she said, "and I would have to stop seeing him." Ever wanting to appear rational and fair, I responded, "I don't think you should let your feelings about me affect your decision." And she didn't.

In a last-ditch effort to hold things together, I persuaded Harold to take a road trip with me to New Orleans while my mother came from Illinois to take care of the girls. There we stayed in a quaint B&B, dined at the Commander's Palace, took a harbor tour and shared beignets at the Café du Monde. In a used bookstore, Harold found and bought *Around the World in 11 Years*, one of the books from my childhood that I had been hunting for years. On the drive home, as I sang all the old blues songs that I had learned on the piano bench beside my mother, he told me I had a lovely voice. But his heart was clearly divided and his mind was far away.

We had agreed that we would separate after our return from New Orleans. But then a friend's daughter announced that she was getting married, and we didn't want to do anything to disrupt the celebratory mood before the wedding, and then my dad's family scheduled a reunion in St. Louis, and Harold, who was fond of all my family, didn't want to miss that. So we limped along for a while until we couldn't do it any more. Throughout all this, the girls had no idea what was going on, although there was at least one occasion when we sat at the dinner table waiting for him to arrive home from work because he had been delayed by walking home with his little friend. Now that I think about it, perhaps how I felt then was how my mother had felt when Dad showed up late for dinner back in those early days in Collinsville.

Finally, one day after work, Harold set the girls down in the living room and told them that we were separating because he was involved with a young woman at work. Sometime after his revelation, not wanting the girls to think that their dad was the only villain in all this, I told them about my affair with the West Indian. In retrospect, I don't know whether my confession made things better or worse. One of our daughters informed me sometime afterwards that she never again knew what to trust as reality; we had seemed like such a stable family. At times when the children were small and I was unhappy with my marriage, I had told myself that I would wait until they were teenagers to separate because I knew they loved their dad and he them, and they deserved to have a good life together. But I learned that, for children, there is really no good time to get divorced—at least in families like ours.

So we separated.

Harold moved to an apartment, and the girls and I stayed in the house. From time to time, he would come back home for clothes or books, and once or twice I visited him in his apartment. I can still remember the warm feeling I had on one of his visits as I saw him striding down the sidewalk toward the house in which we had shared so many good times. Never for a moment did I doubt that I still loved him. But lodged in the pit of my stomach, also, is the memory of finding a letter he had written to his young sweetheart and left lying on the dresser in our bedroom. In it, he told her that he had not been in love with me when we married, but had chosen me because he wanted to have children and a family. As I lay sobbing on the bed in which we had shared some of our best nights, I thought that my worst fears had come true. He had never loved me. I was unlovable. I had made my own bed, and now I was lying in it. Still, we did not divorce for more than a year.

A few months after our separation, knowing how Harold missed his garden and that I had always wanted to live in a condo, where the maintenance was left to others, I suggested that we switch places. Harold came back to the house and Julia and I moved to an apartment in nearby Kettering, where I was now working as editor for the Charles F. Kettering Foundation. Julia transferred to Kettering High School, but Titi, who was a junior, elected to stay with her dad in Dayton View and finish high school at Colonel White. By that time, Tamara was living with her Persian boyfriend and attending Sinclair Community College.

Although Harold often came to see us in the sporty, more youthful clothes his new girlfriend had picked out for him, and her picture was prominently displayed in his apartment, neither he nor I pressed for a divorce. We continued to spend family holidays together for another year, even after Harold moved to Chicago to take a new job while I stayed in Dayton working for the foundation. One fateful day, after I had flown up to Chicago to see if we could possibly patch things up, he said something that made me decide we couldn't go on as we were. We were sitting out on the rooftop that served as a deck for his apartment, discussing our marriage. "I want things to be the way they used to be," he said, "and I think you want things to be different." Sadly, I had to concede that he was right.

Soon afterwards, I filed for dissolution of our marriage. There was no wrangling or blaming; in fact, we shared a lawyer. I asked for no alimony or child support, and we split down the middle the pitifully few assets we had accumulated; Harold even forgave a loan to me of $900 I had used to buy an entertainment center for my new apartment. Informally, he gave me a little money each week while Julia was in high school. Later, at my suggestion, he paid the college expenses for our two older daughters, while I paid for the youngest one until she married in her junior year. Harold had always earned at least twice as much as I, so that seemed like a fair arrangement. I regret now that I did not continue to support Julia after her marriage. Having had the idea drummed into my head from childhood that adult children should be self-supporting once they marry or graduate from college, I took a very hard-nosed stance on self-reliance, forgetting how my parents had helped Harold and me after our marriage by letting us live in their basement apartment.

I have always liked to view myself as an independent thinker, but it was the 1970s, and I was being swept along, largely unconsciously, by a great social tide in American history. It was the age of Gloria Steinem's *Ms.* magazine and Liv Ullmann's autobiography, *Changing*—an age in which people of both sexes were being encouraged to "find themselves" and "fulfill themselves," and I felt that they were talking to me. But despite the many adventures I had in later years, I will always think of the dissolution of my marriage to Harold and the resulting breakup of our family as the end of the most wonderful period of my adult life.

Before I sent this manuscript to the publisher, I sent it to Harold, asking for his feedback and prepared to make changes if necessary, but he declined to read it, saying he preferred to wait for the published book. He told me he trusted me to be honest and fair and that I should be true to myself. "The breaking up of our marriage and our family--it was a truly good marriage in almost every way, and a most wonderful family with bright, interesting and successful children—that was the truly tragic thing," he said. He added that "all the rest of that stuff in the past has taken on the appearance of an old sepia-tone photograph—a little quaint, interesting, perhaps evoking remembered sweetness or sadness, but somewhat ghostlike, insubstantial." I think one of Harold's strengths is that he is able to put the past behind him and savor the present moment, whereas my curse seems to be that the past is almost as real to me as the present, and sometimes more so.

Ronnie, right front, and me behind him with the skating gang from Bethel Tabernacle at the roller rink in Troy, Illinois. This photo was taken in the winter of 1953, about six months before we ran away to Arkansas. I was 14 and he was 20. That's Jeannie, my sexy blond friend, next to me.

Bethel Tabernacle, on 84th Street in East St. Louis, where my parents were co-pastors from 1946 to 1955. The front porch is where I first told Ronnie he was my boyfriend. The sign above the doors announces one of our many "revival" meetings.

The three of us about the time we went on the road, ca. 1941.

Dad with me shortly after my birthday, October 7, 1938.

Don't Get Yourself Talked About

A publicity photo from our time on the road. I was about four in this photo.

Mom and Dad, center top, with the student and faculty musicians from the "Songs of Praise" weekly radio program they presented for Southwestern Bible Institute in Waxahachie, Texas, during the 1945-46 academic year.

Dad, center, with Mom on his left, in front of the Southwestern Bible Institute Auditorium with students and faculty participants in the "Songs of Praise" radio program.

Grandma and Grandpa Chamless with Dad and his little brother, Ezra, who died in infancy.

Don't Get Yourself Talked About

My paternal grandmother, Etta Julia Thurman,
before she married my grandfather.

Dad and Mom, both at 17, before they met.

Pat Piety

Dad, second from left center, in the sweater and tie. Already a preacher for four years, he was 19 in this photo. His dad, also a preacher, is second from left in the right section, wearing the gray suit.

Mom, right front, with her parents and seven younger siblings. Aunt Bess (Carolyn) is front left, Uncle Jim back right, and Aunt Edith is in the middle.

Don't Get Yourself Talked About

Dad, far left, with Uncle Joel, Grandpa Chamless, Uncle James, and Uncle Wes (also known as "Titus" in his youth). Dad was six feet tall and 175 pounds, but Uncle Wes was a giant by comparison.

Me with brother John in his playpen outside our house in Collinsville. I was nine years old.

Dad, John and Mom. I don't know why this studio portrait was taken or why I wasn't in it, and John doesn't remember. I was probably on vacation in Texas with Ray. It must have been about the time I overheard Mom say to Dad, "John is all I have in the world."

Ray's abandoned house in Electra, Texas, in the early 1970s, after she had died. When I went inside, I found the painted parrot still hanging by the door where I remembered her sitting to talk on the phone.

Don't Get Yourself Talked About

The church in Electra, across the street from Ray's house. When we lived there, the parsonage was on the far side. The front section, which was originally a porch, was added on after we left. An oil town, Electra stayed virtually unchanged for many years after the oil ran out.

Dad, John, and Aunt Wanda Fay in Forest Park in St. Louis, shortly after I had come home from the failed elopement

Our wedding night, January 25, 1958. Some people thought I was older than Harold, but he was seven years my senior.

With Mom, Grandma Chamless, and Grandma Rainbolt, later that same evening.

Don't Get Yourself Talked About

Harold and I show off our firstborn to Dad, Mom and my Rainbolt grandparents, Christmas 1958.

Our three darling little girls, "Tammy," "Titi" and "Julie," in dresses I made for them. I wasn't much of a seamstress. I also cut their hair.

Pat Piety

Tamara, Titi, and Julia, in 1978, about the time Harold and I separated.

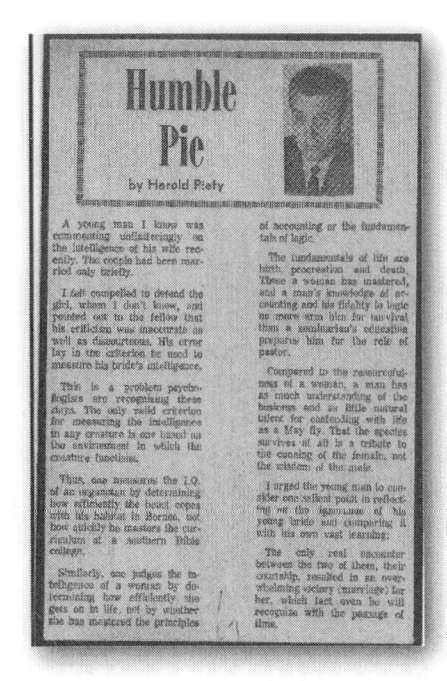

Harold's column in the now-defunct *Metro-East Journal*, wherein he explains his views on men, women and marriage.

Don't Get Yourself Talked About

Mom in Asuncion, Paraguay, in January 1979, shortly after her 67th birthday.

The international airport in Asuncion where Mom and her colleagues from the Academy were waiting to greet me when I arrived in January 1979.

Mom and her students at the Academy.

Dad at a church somewhere in Mexico in the mid-1960s. He went down there alone to try out his Spanish—and perhaps consider living there.

Don't Get Yourself Talked About

Me with brother John, sometime in the late 1960s or early 1970s.

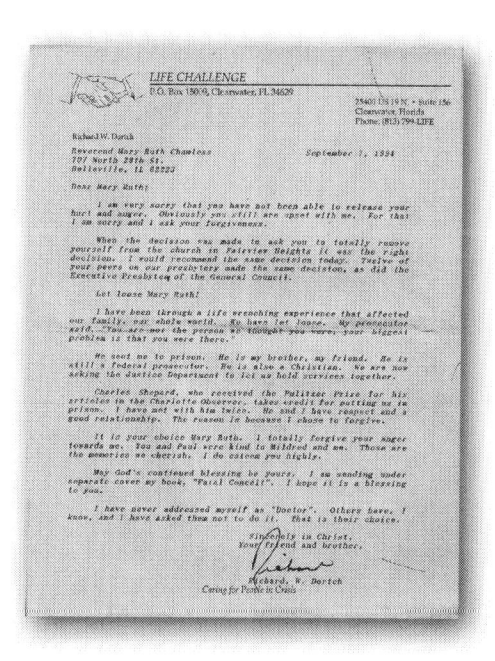

Letter to Mom, along with book and flyleaf inscription from her old frenemy, Richard Dortch, who was sentenced to prison for financial fraud in connection with Jim Bakker's "PTL Club" a few years after he had presided over a meeting in which Mom was deprived of her papers as an ordained Assemblies of God minister.

From the best-selling author of Integrity
FATAL
CONCEIT
A Bold Challenge to
Everyone in This
Power-Hungry World
Richard W. Dortch
Former President of PTL

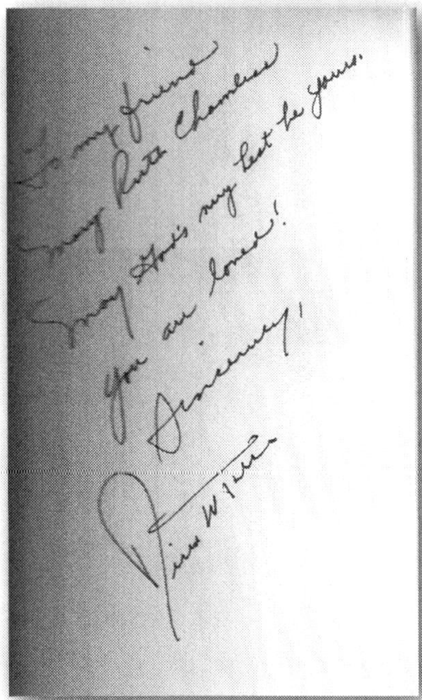

Don't Get Yourself Talked About

Family reunion photo in the yard behind my house in Stillwater, Oklahoma, 2004. Harold and his wife, Christine, left; brother John and his wife, Kathryn, next; Brian Foley, Titi's husband, in dark shirt; Phillip Rieman, Julia's husband, in striped shirt; and me, back row. Tamara, Titi (Marilyn) and Julia are on the bench.

My beloved little house and big yard in Stillwater, Oklahoma, where I moved after Mom's death in 2003.

Uncle Wes and Aunt Louise. Among other things, Uncle Wes was a photographer, so he probably took this photo himself.

Mom's book about the history of women ministers in the Assemblies of God movement from 1914 to 1934. She devoted more than five years to the research, included an index, and published it herself. It sold nearly 2,000 copies. The drawing on the cover is by daughter Marilyn Piety Foley, her granddaughter, who is also known as "Titi" and, professionally, M.G. Piety.

For most of my life, I have been a half-conscious believer in the "pathetic fallacy"—the idea that, in fiction at least, Nature mirrors the protagonist's emotions—and I've had no trouble in finding support for my irrational belief. On March 28, 1979, just a few months after my marriage was officially dissolved, one of the two nuclear reactors at Three Mile Island in Pennsylvania suffered a partial meltdown and Harold, who was by then working as an account executive for the public relations firm of Hill and Knowlton in Chicago, was sent to handle media relations for the Pennsylvania Electric Association, which was in charge of Three Mile Island. That same year, La Soufrière, an active volcano on the West Indian island of St. Vincent, erupted immediately after my West Indian lover returned to his home there. In my mind, God was venting his wrath for my profligate behavior by putting two men I loved in harm's way. I'm sure this sounds completely absurd to anyone who has a less histrionic imagination or who was not brought up in a religion that emphasized in vivid detail God's punishment of sinners, but it was painfully real to me. Some people think they are the center of the universe. Apparently, I have thought that a lot of times in my life—especially when bad things happen to people I care about.

For many years after our divorce I suffered from periodic bouts of deep depression in which I blamed my wayward sexual behavior and selfishness for the dissolution of our marriage, the harm it had done to our children, and the breakup of the family that had meant so much to me. And although I had several intense and exciting relationships with men in later years and was married briefly to another man, I never stopped feeling married to Harold. Perhaps that's why the men I fell in love with in later life were not the least bit like either Harold or my dad, and our relationships never came close to ending in marriage. I realized, eventually, that I was attracted to men who had qualities I admired, and that I thought I lacked.

Before those later adventures, though, I did marry again, in 1982, a year after Harold married Christine, the woman who has now been his loving wife for more than 30 years (not the teenager he had left me for). I did it partly because I realized there was no hope of rebuilding the family I had lost, but also to please my mother and my future mother-in-law, both of whom were very religious and extremely embarrassed that their children were living together "in sin." In this marriage, I felt more like an equal partner. We were married in San Miguel de Allende, Mexico, on one of our many road trips. My new husband and I had good times together, riding bicycles along the Dayton riverfront, taking long motor trips through the Southwest and Mexico, and spending several memorable weekends in New York City. He was a marathon runner, and I enjoyed watching him run. Often I was moved to tears by the spirit of the marathons, in which even runners who came in last were cheered by strangers on the sidelines for giving their best. It seemed to me that marathons brought out the best in people, unlike team sports, which force players and fans to choose sides.

My new husband was also fond of mountain climbing, and he was champing at the bit to move out west, where there was something to climb. Growing weary of the rainy, overcast Dayton winters, I agreed that perhaps it was time to move to a sunnier climate, so I dreamed up a plan: I would go out to Sun City, Arizona, where his parents lived, and house-sit for them while they went away for the summer, during which time I would try to do some freelance writing and look for a job. When I found work, he could quit his job in Dayton, come out to join me, and look for a new job in Phoenix.

The first part of the plan worked liked a charm. Although I didn't find any freelance assignments, I did find a job rather quickly in the public affairs department of the Western Region Operations Center of American

Express. At Kettering, I had researched and written the script for a documentary film on the famous inventor, Charles F. Kettering, called *Boss Ket: One Man, Working With Others*, which was narrated by E.G. Marshall and shown on local PBS stations. I shared the film with my interviewer at American Express and was hired immediately at a salary a couple thousand dollars higher than my salary at Kettering. The company even paid my moving expenses from Dayton, an unexpected bonus! I arrived in Phoenix in mid-May, and by July 3, 1983, I was working for American Express. Things were looking up.

I have always had anxiety about working for other people. It's not so much that I think I can't perform well; it's more that I'm not confident of how my performance will be perceived by my superiors. If I had to guess a reason for this anxiety, I would trace it back to those early days with Mom, when nothing I did seemed to be right, or maybe from that traumatic appearance before the presbyters on my fifteenth birthday. But the truth is that my mother also had a lot of nervous problems, so anxiety may be in my genes. In any case, although I had thought of my job at the Kettering Foundation as stressful, especially at first, I found myself singularly unprepared for the stress endemic to working for a high-profile international corporation like American Express. My new husband had decided to stay back in Dayton and accumulate a little more money before joining me, so I was alone in those first few months in Phoenix. Filled with anxiety about my ability to perform, I felt a frequent fluttering in my chest, and one day, lying on the floor of the apartment I had rented for the two of us before our furniture arrived, I felt the carotid artery in my neck and noticed that my heartbeat seemed irregular.

Through the phone book, I found a doctor, who hooked me up to an electrocardiograph machine, which confirmed my suspicions. "It's just stress," I told him, remembering how stressed I had felt at other times in my life. "Give me some tranquilizers, and I'll be OK." But the doctor disagreed. Stress could aggravate my condition, he said, but it couldn't cause it, so he prescribed a heart regulator called Quinaglute. Before going to the doctor, I had not felt any pain—just the fluttering in my chest—but after starting the medicine, I began to feel intense chest pain. I still had to work long hours every day—I didn't dare ask for time off after being so recently hired—but sometimes when I came home from work, I would lean over the steering wheel in the parking lot, too tired and in pain to get up and go into the apartment. So my doctor sent me to the Arizona Heart Institute, where I flunked all of the stress tests and had to have my heart catheterized. "Oh," the doctors said when they looked at the results, "your arteries look very good. They must constrict when you are under stress." Despite their conclusion, my phone book doctor wanted to put me on nitroglycerin for the chest pain, which had come only after he had given me the Quinaglute. Deciding that he was a quack, and that I would rather die of a heart attack than go on feeling the way I did, I dropped that doctor and began to wean myself off the medicine by gradually cutting the dosage.

In the meantime, when my new husband finally joined me in Phoenix, I learned that he had fallen in love with a co-worker back in Dayton while I was out West. Trying to learn from my mistakes, I had promised myself that in my new marriage I would be faithful for the rest of my life, but during the most tender moments with him, sometimes I would cry silently, remembering my first marriage and the family I had lost, so I could understand why my second husband had fallen in love with someone else. My heart was still with Harold and the life we had built together.

Still firmly convinced that you can't make anyone love you, I didn't fight to save this marriage. But I couldn't stand to sleep in our bed alone, so I spent nights on the couch in the living room, pretending that the back was another human being, holding me. During our separation, my husband's father had told me part of the problem was that I loved my children too much. To me, it seemed like an absurd statement. How can you love your children too much? In later years, I have come to understand that love and attachment are not necessarily the same, so perhaps I *was* too attached to my children and my memories of the past. In any case, the day I signed the papers for my second divorce (I didn't even get a lawyer or go to court—just told him to handle everything), I was all alone and stuck in a stressful job in Phoenix, a thousand miles from my nearest relative. I had no financial reserves that would allow me to quit work and return home, and I had no idea where my life would go next. I felt like a total failure.

Sometimes one has no choice but to go on, so I went on. And, in time, things got a lot better. The tyrant who had been senior VP of the center when I came on board was summarily moved to another division, which the company sold within six months. The new senior VP, having heard that I was a speechwriter, asked me to write for him, and the relationship proved very rewarding. Together with a young typesetter at the center, I also started a new employee newsletter that went to several thousand employees and was well received. Things were definitely looking up.

Approximately a decade before my divorce from Harold, my parents' marriage of 34 years had also come to an end. Despite the fact that, according to Dad, their relationship had enjoyed a brief burst of renewed passion while Dad was traveling and raising money for Evangel College, the years when he tried to make a living selling books had taken a toll on their relationship. Dad's income from the bookstore had to be supplemented in other ways. I don't know how much he made from all of his ventures, but I believe he got more from dealing in rare books by mail—and tinting, matting, and framing antique prints for sale—than he did from the bookstore, even after he moved it downtown to Collinsville Avenue. I know that a year and a half after my marriage to Harold, Dad supplemented his income by helping my mother's brothers build our first house for us. But all of his efforts did not bring in enough money to equal what Mom was earning as a schoolteacher, and, according to my brother, who was still living at home, Mom never let Dad forget it.

What really caused havoc in the family, though, was that Dad, perhaps emboldened by Harold's non-religious views, decided to start attending the First Unitarian Church of St. Louis and, later, the Ethical Society. Although Dad's views had been more fundamentalist than Mom's when he first met her, all of his reading and experience over the years had caused him gradually to develop more liberal attitudes toward religion. He never abandoned the principles set forth by Jesus in the Sermon on the Mount, but it was pretty clear that he had some serious doubts about a lot of the other claims in the Bible. And while Mom had never been the stereotypical shouting, talking-in-tongues kind of Pentecostal (she was much too concerned about appearances for such blatant emotionality, despite her outbursts at home), she held fast to her church and was both embarrassed and defensive about Dad's ventures onto less hallowed ground. In fact, she made life a living hell for all of us about it. She hated the Unitarians and the Ethical Society—"secular humanists," she called them, as if that term put them in a class with murderers or at least "stupid" people—and although Harold and I were attending the Unitarian Church during that time, I had some sympathy for her when I learned that one of the leaders of these groups had told her that religions like hers were "products of ignorance and superstition." It's hard to imagine anyone who considers himself intelligent and ethical making such an ignorant and insensitive statement to a believer.

In many ways, Mom was a very conscientious and giving person. She made quilts for all of her siblings, her children and her grandchildren, and she encouraged several female friends and relatives to go back to school and become teachers, thereby exerting a positive influence on their lives. She even gave some of them a little money from time to time, I think. I have met at least one person who said she was one of their favorite teachers, so I'm sure some people would be shocked to see how cruel she could be to people in her immediate family. During this period when Mom was so upset with Dad for his forays into other approaches to religion and ethics, we were having a pleasant discussion at my house when I said something to the effect that, despite the problems between us when I was growing up, I was glad we had become friends. A few days later, I received a very painful letter from her, in which she wrote, "I am NOT your friend! I am your mother, and I'm tired of this crap!" She didn't detail what "crap" she was talking about, but it was obvious that she meant the business of Dad's straying from the religious fold, for which she held me, and my husband, partially responsible.

As they often did in matters concerning blood relatives, Mom's family got involved, too. In the middle of all this wrangling, Aunt Edith invited Mom to Thanksgiving dinner, explicitly not inviting Dad. And my grandmother, from whom Mom had obviously acquired her talent for writing poison pen letters, sent Harold a letter in which she blamed him for Dad's wayward behavior. "Ever since you came into the family there has been trouble," she wrote, adding, "Why don't you try sleeping in the garage for awhile?" This struck me as terribly unfair and unkind; if anything, Harold was more attached to my extended family than I was, learning the names of my great aunts and uncles and second cousins, basking for the first time in the warmth of a large family. I was so hurt and angry on his behalf that I didn't speak to my grandmother for a year, relenting only when she visited me in the hospital when I was ill.

Although Mom had often railed at Dad for being a hypocrite for not believing every word of the Bible while he was pastoring the church in East St. Louis, she reversed course 180 degrees when he started going to the Unitarian Church. "Why don't you admit that you believe?" she would accost him. "I wish you would just find a little church somewhere so we could go back to pastoring." According to Dad, she even sent a letter to the board of the local philharmonic orchestra on which he served, saying she was tired of her husband hanging around with "all those drunks" on the board. To Dad's intense embarrassment, the letter had to be shared with the board members. Another time, when she saw his car outside a restaurant where he was allegedly attending a board meeting, she got in his car and drove it several blocks past her own, walked back to get her car, drove it past his, and walked back to get his, repeating the process until she got both cars to their home, up a very steep hill a couple of miles away. When he came out of the restaurant, he thought his car had been stolen. She thought it was funny. In retrospect, such tales seem funny to me, too, but they were no joke at the time.

Dad and I sometimes talked about Mom's erratic behavior, and while it was obvious that it hurt him deeply, he believed she was a victim of some mental or emotional disorder beyond her control. "She's like a blind person," he said. After a year or two, though, he caved under all the pressure and found a little church in a tiny town in central Illinois called Sorento, where he was elected pastor. He served there for several years, so popular with both members and townsfolk that he even had a regular column in the local newspaper. The church came with a parsonage, but Mom didn't want to give up her job in East St. Louis, and John, who was a junior in high school, didn't want to stop attending school in Belleville, so the two of them drove the 55 miles from Sorento to East St. Louis, by way of Belleville, five days a week during the next couple of school years.

Before we moved to Ohio, Harold and I had occasionally brought the girls up to Sorento on weekends to visit their grandparents. One Sunday after church, when we were all sharing a noon meal at a restaurant in nearby Greenville, the discussion turned to William Jennings Bryan. I didn't know enough to make many comments, but Dad, Harold and John, who was home from college for the weekend, were making fun of Bryan as being a sanctimonious and cynical politician. Mom was defending him, and finally, she got so mad that she went back to the house in Sorento, packed up her stuff and moved back to Belleville. While she was packing, our daughter Tammy, who was about 6 years old, was very worried, so I took her aside and said, "Honey, don't worry. Grandma has done this before. She'll come back." Still worried, Tammy followed her Grandmother around the house as she packed. After a while, she said, loud enough for Mom to hear, "Mom, did she take her sewing machine when she left the other times? She's taking her sewing machine!" Again, the story is funny in retrospect, but it was not so funny at the time.

The house in Belleville had an efficiency apartment in the walk-out basement for evangelists who used to come to hold "revival" meetings at Bethel Tabernacle, so after the blow-up, Mom moved into it temporarily, informing the renters upstairs that they had 30 days to find another home. Thereafter, Mom came back to Sorento on weekends to play for Sunday services. She and Dad eventually made up, sort of, but their relationship was pretty much downhill after that. Whenever Dad found a book that he liked to read that didn't have special resale value, he would keep it, underlining passages he liked, listing the page numbers of his favorite poems, and often writing comments in the margins and the front of the book. After his death, I inherited several of these books, in which I found cryptic messages about Dad's feelings regarding life with Mom. In one volume, a collection of poems by Margaret Fishback called *One to a Customer*, he had written "Bought in Des Moines, Iowa, Sept. 1965 . . . Sad, Sad Memories!" Less than five years later, Mom divorced Dad to "teach him a lesson," so she said, although she never told me what the lesson was supposed to be.

After my parents' divorce, Dad gave up the church in Sorento and moved to Edwardsville, where he had been working on contract as a book scout for the new library at the emerging Edwardsville branch of Southern Illinois University. He had been trying to learn Spanish for several years, driving around listening to tape-recorded messages, and I think it was during this time, or perhaps while he and Mom were still estranged, that he took a long solo drive into the Yucatan Peninsula of Mexico, stopping at little churches along the way to preach in halting Spanish. But he got a severe intestinal disorder and had to be hospitalized, after which he returned home and apparently gave up on Spanish. I never found out whether he had harbored a secret ambition of moving to Mexico and pastoring a little church there, but it would be ironic if he had, considering Mom's adventure with another Spanish-speaking country later on.

Dad protested until the end that he didn't want a divorce—he even sent me a copy of a letter from his lawyer saying as much—and after the divorce, he swore that he would never marry again. But within less than two years, he married one of Mom's closest friends from the church in Sorento. I sometimes wonder if Mom ever thought about the fact that if she had not insisted that Dad should go back to preaching, he never would have met her replacement.

For several years after Dad's remarriage, Mom cried, railed and took tranquilizers, seeming half out of her mind at times. She went on teaching for a few more years, but she told me later that she finally decided to retire when she lost control one day and gave a little boy a hard whipping. "He was a good little boy," she recalled sadly, "but I had warned the kids that the next one who caused a problem was going to get a spanking, and he happened to be the one." She never got over feeling guilty about what she had done to that little boy.

She never got over Dad's marriage to her friend, either, but she refused to accept any blame for that. When Dad married again, I had a lot of anxiety about how to handle the situation. Mom's family had pretty much of a "Hatfields and McCoys" approach to differences with those not related by blood who had offended them in some way. Like many women whose husbands have remarried, she was eager to place a large share of the blame on the "other woman," although I had never seen any evidence that Dad had been involved with his second wife during his marriage to Mom, nor had Mom ever hinted at it while she was still married to Dad. Knowing Mom, I was pretty certain she would have made her suspicions known at the time.

There was one complication, though: That ESP thing Dad and I had. Once while he was living alone in Edwardsville after the divorce, I spent the night at his apartment and we stayed up very late, even though we were scheduled to get up around dawn the next day to take a trip somewhere. As I was passing by his bedroom, I heard him talking to someone on the phone, asking that person to wake him in the morning. "Who in the world could he call at this time of night to ask something like that?" I thought, and the answer came to me in an instant: It had to be Mom's friend. She had always been a caretaker, even coming to babysit my girls once when they had chickenpox while she and Mom were still friends. She was just the kind of person people called when they were in need, and she obviously enjoyed being there for them. So when Dad came to visit us in Ohio a few months later and announced happily, "I'm going to get married, and you'll never guess who!" I immediately responded with the name of Mom's friend. The look on his face was priceless; he thought he had kept the whole thing a secret, and he was flabbergasted that I had figured it out.

My concern over Dad's remarriage and Mom's subsequent breakdown was even more complicated by the fact that during the years I was growing up, I had periodically suggested divorce to both of them. They were apparently so unhappy together, I thought it was obvious they would be happier apart. Which only shows how little outsiders can know about a marriage.

So when Dad and his new wife came to spend their first Christmas with our family in Ohio, I could barely function. I had never suffered from hives before and have never had them since, but I had a terrible case while Dad and my new stepmother were visiting. I tried to blame it on a food allergy, but I must have known in my heart that it was caused by sheer terror of what my mother would do when she discovered that I had entertained Dad and "the other woman" under my own roof. And I had good reason to be scared.

The next Christmas, when Aunt Edith and Mom came to visit us in Ohio, Mom was still weeping and moping like a diva in some tragic opera, both around the house and during the Christmas service at the Church of the Brethren, where we took her and her sister. Not knowing what to do or say, I tried not to notice. I figured if I inquired what was wrong, I would be inundated by stories of malicious betrayal, and required to take sides. Finally, Aunt Edith decided to take the bull by the horns:

"Pat, if your mother doesn't get better, we're going to have to go home."

I figured she was begging me to ask what was the matter and looking forward with relish to a good session of trashing Dad and my stepmother, during which exchange I would be pressured to take Mom's side. So, trying to dodge the bullet, I replied lamely, "Well, OK."

That was a big mistake.

Immediately, Aunt Edith began packing their bags and returning the Christmas presents we had given to her and Mom. As they stood in the doorway preparing to leave for home, Mom, in tears, shook her finger at me, exclaiming loudly, "It was you! It was you! It was you!"

Still carrying a heavy load of guilt about how my youthful misadventure had torn our church apart and caused my parents so many problems, I couldn't escape the feeling that, somehow, I *was* guilty—that, in fact, I might just be guilty for all of the suffering in the world, everywhere. My daughters have often assured me that I am not the center of the universe, and that I am neither the cause of everything that goes wrong nor the person who can make everything right, but it's sometimes hard to believe them when I remember how much damage I caused as a teenager.

After Dad's marriage, Mom tried to avoid going anywhere that people might remember her past or ask questions about her divorce. She joined a new congregation in which most of the people had not known her during her previous incarnations. And while she was not the minister in that church, she did become its secretary, in which position she was charged with taking minutes for the board meetings. It was the 1970s, televangelism was taking off like a rocket, and the Assemblies of God movement, in Mom's view, was experiencing growth fever. The leaders of the group of loosely affiliated "assemblies" that had once been ridiculed as "Holy Rollers" now saw their chance to gain some respect by increasing the movement's numbers, and one way they did so was by pulling more independent congregations into the association, combining them to make bigger ones. In line with that thinking, the presbyters in charge of the district where Mom's church was located were inspired to merge her church, which was affiliated with the Assemblies of God, with another congregation that wasn't—and without asking permission of the local church deacons.

Above all else, Mom was a fighter, and before long she found herself in another fight with the dreaded presbyters. I didn't witness any of this confrontation first-hand, so I can only relay what Mom told me, but it seemed to me that she was in the right on this issue. When she refused to hand over the church minutes, saying it was against the by-laws, she was called before a hearing with the presbyters, and they took away her minister's papers. She was in her 60s by then and had been preaching since her early 20s, so it had to be a terrible blow. To make matters worse, the head presbyter in this group had long been a friend to Mom and Dad, although I was only familiar with his name: Richard Dortch. This name would pop up very dramatically in the national news a few years later, but at the time of Mom's hearing, "Dick" was riding high and did not hesitate to wield his authority against his old friend. The unkindest cut of all, though, may have been when another one of the presbyters suggested that it was time for Mom to take to her rocking chair and let the younger ones take over leadership of the movement. If he had known Mom better, I'm pretty sure he would not have made such a remark.

I kept waiting for Mom to break down altogether after she was kicked out of the ministry, but she seemed to take it a lot better than expected. She was upset and embarrassed, of course, and for a while she avoided going anywhere she might meet Assemblies of God people from her past, but she seemed to be holding up pretty well.

And then she made a move that took us all by surprise.

Hearing a missionary speak one night about an interdenominational English-language school in Asuncion, Paraguay, Mom decided to sell her car, rent her house, and take a job as a teacher at Asuncion Christian Academy. She was 66 years old, her knowledge of Spanish was rudimentary at best, and she didn't know anyone in Paraguay. My divorce from Harold had recently been finalized, and Julia and I were living in the apartment in Kettering, Ohio. When Mom told me she was thinking of going to teach in Paraguay, I promised her that if she went, I would visit her there. She did, and I did.

I got to Asuncion in time to help Mom celebrate her 67th birthday on January 29, 1979. She was renting a room and bath in a doctor's home that had a lovely swimming pool in the back yard, complete with waterfall, that one of the doctor's patients had constructed as payment for medical treatments. It was the middle of summer in Paraguay, so to welcome me to Asuncion and introduce me to her landlord's family and her colleagues at the school, Mom hosted a pool party there. She didn't go in the water herself (the only time I had ever seen her in a bathing suit was when we had taken all-female water exercise classes together at the YMCA in Granite

City, Illinois, years before), but *I* went swimming, and so did many of the guests, who had a great time.

Without a car, Mom walked everywhere in Asuncion, and, as a result, she lost 20 pounds and gained some color in the bright Paraguayan sun. Best of all, she seemed happier than I had seen her in the 30 years since we had left Waxahachie. In many ways, her time in Asuncion was a return to the life she had loved back then: She taught math and music, and her students and colleagues were obviously very fond of her. In fact, a whole gang of them was waiting on the balcony of the tiny Asuncion airport when I arrived. The faculty, which came from all over the world, formed a tight little social group much like Mom's former associates in Waxahachie had done. They threw parties, went out to dinner together, and took car trips to places as far away as Uruguay and Brazil. While I was visiting, a couple of Mom's friends took us on motor trips—one to the famous Iguazu Falls, on the border between Paraguay, Argentina and Brazil, and another to a scenic village on the bank of San Bernardino Lake, the largest lake in Paraguay. Later on, after I left, Mom even directed a musical production of *Tom Sawyer*, for which the students presented her with a large, elaborate certificate of appreciation. At Christmas time, her students presented a musical program at the American Embassy.

One day while we were sitting on the doctor's porch talking, Mom confessed to me that her decision to go to Paraguay had originally been a "suicidal" gesture born of her depression over Dad's remarriage and the loss of her minister's papers with the Assemblies of God. "I thought I would leave everything behind, go where no one knew me and just fade away," she said. But, instead, her virtual suicide plan turned out to be one of the greatest adventures of her life.

Despite how happy she was, though, she decided to return home to Illinois after a year of teaching in Asuncion. Part of the reason might have been anxiety about living in a country that was still a dictatorship under the notorious Alberto Stroessner. While the country was virtually crime free, those who crossed Alberto in any way did not fare well, so there was a vague undercurrent of tension in the air. As we were driving past the jail in Asuncion during my visit, one of her friends in the car remarked, "We used to hear the cries of the prisoners being tortured there, but the building has been soundproofed, so we don't hear them anymore." (I had naively expected him to say "but they don't do that anymore.") I suspect, though, that Mom's family had a lot to do with her decision to return home. Except for her sister Carolyn, who had been a missionary over much of Asia, I think the rest of Mom's family had not been very supportive of her plan to go to Paraguay in the first place. She told me with obvious resentment that when her brother Bob had driven her to the airport for her flight to Paraguay, he had asked, "If you die down there, do you want to be buried there or have your body shipped home?"

The faculty and her students at the Academy didn't want to let Mom go, and for the next year after her return to the States, they kept writing and asking her to come back. So after a year's break, she returned to Asuncion to resume teaching. Unfortunately, her second stint did not go as smoothly as the first. Shortly after I wrote to tell her I was living with the man who would later become my second husband, she was hospitalized with high blood pressure, thereby reinforcing my impression that I still possessed exceptional negative powers over other people's lives.

Another rather unpleasant event during her second stay was the assassination of exiled former Nicaraguan dictator Anastasio Somoza Debayle, which occurred on September 17, 1980, not far from the Asuncion Academy. Mom and the other people at the school heard the attack, which, according to reports, involved a seven-person team armed with AK-47 rifles, automatic pistols, and an RPG-7 rocket launcher with four anti-tank grenades and two rockets. After the assassination, Mom and the other American faculty members were rounded up and taken to the American Embassy for fingerprinting, just in case.

As Christmas approached, Mom's sister Edith wrote several times asking her to come home for the holidays. Not wanting to spend the extra money, Mom told her to be patient—that she would be home in a few months. Unfortunately, Aunt Edith died of a sudden heart attack shortly after Christmas, and Mom, conscience-stricken for not responding to her sister's pleas, returned home for the funeral, never to return to Asuncion. For several years after her return, though, her coworkers and students continued to write to her, begging her to come back.

When I was in my late 40s, I heard something that made me see my relationship with Mom in a new way. For most of my adult life I have attended counseling, off and on. Usually, the counselors have just listened or asked questions, seldom commenting or offering opinions. But once when I was talking to the head of behavioral medicine at Good Samaritan Hospital in Phoenix about a book my middle daughter had sent me, he said something that made me think about my life in a new way. The book was *The Art of Loving*, by Eric Fromm. "Fromm defines two kinds of love," I told the doctor. "He says maternal love is the kind you get for simply being yourself, whereas paternal love is the kind you get for living up to expectations. But that wasn't my experience. I never doubted my Dad's love, but I felt that I didn't live up to my mother's expectations."

"That's because your mother was chronically depressed," he said. "Children of chronically depressed parents often feel they are somehow to blame. They keep trying to make their parents happy, and they feel like failures when they don't succeed."

His comment made me think of the many ways I had tried to make my mother feel better throughout my life, even during those periods when we were so often at swords' points with each other. I recalled how she had told me that, when I was a preschooler, sometimes she would be left at home with a "sick headache" while Dad was out with his friends after church, and I would bring her wet cloths for her head. I don't remember those times, but I do remember that, as I got older, she had frequent headaches and I was the one she relied on for a good neck and shoulder rub. She didn't mind how hard I dug my palms and knuckles into those tight muscles, and when I gripped her head in both hands and slowly but firmly pulled up on it, she said it relieved some of the pain. At other times, I would put her hair up on curlers and comb it out in new "do's" or make up her face for fun, even though she never wore makeup in public. From the infinite wisdom of my experience as a teenager and young adult, I even gave her little lectures on happiness: "The way to get love is to give it," I would tell her when she said, as she often did, "All I ever wanted was someone to love me for myself."

There was no doubt that I had always loved her and wanted her to be happy, even as I nursed some deep resentments against her. And after our good time together in Paraguay, when she confessed that her move down there had been a "suicidal impulse," we began to grow closer. Since I was scheduled to stop in Rio de Janeiro on my way home from Asuncion, I decided to give her a special treat by flying her to Rio with me, where we spent a couple of nights in the swanky Intercontinental Hotel before she went back to Asuncion and I flew on home to the States. We had a great time in Rio, fantasizing that we were members of the jet set like the women we saw sashaying around the pool in their bikinis and sarongs, and once, as we were riding a van into downtown Rio to meet a Palestinian man who had promised to take us to dinner (he was the brother of some friends in Dayton), I gave her a shock. Gazing out the window, I saw a man standing under the overpass, smoking a cigarette. Feeling frisky and safe from any possible consequences, I gave him a flirty look, at which he dropped his cigarette and stared at me. Mom, who was sitting in the aisle seat, couldn't see my face, but she saw his startled response. "What did you do to him?!" she asked. I could tell that she was a little titillated by the thought that I had flirted so blatantly with a stranger, and during that trip I began to suspect that, despite her rather Puritanical exterior, I was actually an alter ego for the wild side she usually kept so carefully in check. After all, *I* wasn't the one who had danced with a bucket of beer on my head as a teenager.

Shortly after Mom came home from Paraguay, I moved to Phoenix, Arizona. Since I was going out alone, leaving my new husband to hold down a job until I could find one out west, Mom drove with me to help move, and on the way she talked a lot about her early days as a preacher and the many women preachers she had known during the 1930s and '40s. "Someone ought to write a book about them," she declared, noting that the number of women preachers in the Assemblies of God had clearly been on the decline for several years. "Why don't you write it?" I suggested, promising that I would edit it for her. And that's exactly what she proceeded to do. For the next five years, she worked diligently at researching the history of women ministers in the Assemblies of God movement, driving down to study the official rolls of ministers and other historical documents in the central archives in Springfield, Missouri.

In addition, she wrote to and interviewed many women on the list, tracking down all she could find, and asking them for anecdotes and photos. She received some very interesting responses, all of which she included in her book. She also charted the rise and decline in the percentage of women ministers in the movement from 1914 to 1934 and made graphs for the book. And even though by this time she had been divorced from Dad for well over a decade, she gave him credit in the introduction for encouraging her to continue preaching after their marriage:

When we married, I told Paul that I would play and sing, but that he would be the preacher. That arrangement suited Paul fine until he realized that I meant it. I refused all his offers to speak at any of the services. After some time in Terrell [the first church Dad pastored after their marriage], he asked me to take the service because he had to go to Dallas and would be unable to get back in time for services, so I finally consented. I had a good service and an enthusiastic audience while Paul sat outside the building (unknown to me) and listened to me speak.

Behold God's Handmaid, by Mary Ruth Chamless

By the time they took the church in East St. Louis, though, Mom had obviously changed her mind about taking a back seat to Dad, since I often heard her remind him angrily that they had been elected co-pastors. She always vehemently denied that she was a feminist, but, as far as I am concerned, she was the first feminist in my life. When I was growing up, as soon as she started teaching school, she bought her own car and established her own checking account, and I once heard her bawl Dad out for opening her mail. Occasionally during their marriage, Mom would say that all she wanted was a strong man who would take charge of things. Picturing her in my head as a fierce lioness, I would joke, "Mom, he would need a whip and a chair!"

After working on the book for five years, Mom self-published *Behold God's Handmaid* in 1988, and I created a brochure for her, which she mailed out to Assemblies of God women all over the country. The icing on the cake was that her book was advertised and sold through the catalog of the Assemblies of God's Gospel Publishing House in Springfield, Illinois. So several years after having been summarily thrown out of the ministry by the presbyters and advised to take to her rocking chair, Mom had achieved the ultimate vindication. But she had many more years to live after publishing her book—years in which she would gain even more vindication, I would learn a lot more about her, and we would both discover some surprising facts connected with my long-ago elopement and what had become of the boy I ran away with.

When Dad remarried, he was no longer able to serve as an Assemblies of God minister. But he continued to preach occasionally at small independent congregations on the Missouri side of the Mississippi. By that time, he had established a working relationship with the emerging Lovejoy Library at Southern Illinois University in Edwardsville, which was trying to build its collection. At first he was a "book scout" on contract, but soon he joined the staff as a full-time "field representative," a position that was invented for this man with almost no formal education but an impressive amount of expertise on rare and valuable books. From what he told me, his second marriage was a lot more peaceful than the first, and he was a good second father to his two stepsons. When he developed Alzheimer's in his late 60s, my stepmother took excellent care of him.

During the years that Dad's Alzheimer's was gradually worsening, I was working in public affairs for American Express in Phoenix, and he would come to stay with me for a week or more at a time before his illness made it impossible for him to travel unassisted or be left at home while I was at work. Once when he and my stepmother came for a visit, I took them for a drive to see some of the fancy resorts and beautiful homes in that desert city, but Dad wasn't interested. "Take me to where the poor people live," he said. All through my growing-up years, Dad had been the nurturing parent, placing books on my shelves that reinforced, with varying degrees of subtlety, the great values of compassion, humility and empathy that made him such a good counselor and confidant in his role as minister. He had never forgotten the poverty of his youth, and although he had acquired a number of affluent friends in the process of collecting rare books and selling prints of grand historic homesteads to the former owners' descendants, his heart was always with the poor, the downtrodden and the outcast.

When he came alone to visit me in Phoenix, we would often take walks in the evening after I got home from work. He couldn't remember why I was in Phoenix and kept asking me, every few minutes, "How did you get to Phoenix?" whereupon, I would patiently explain. Finally, though, my patience gave out and I answered testily, "Dad, I've told you a dozen times!" Instantly regretting my words, I said, "Oh, Dad, I'm so sorry. I wouldn't hurt you for the world," to which he replied, "Oh, that's OK—I won't remember it." He never lost his sense of humor.

During one of these walks, when I was in the middle of becoming divorced from my second husband, Dad reached out to me in a way that I will never forget. Despite his obvious confusion about a lot of things, he apparently sensed that I was upset about the divorce and trying to hide it, because he suddenly burst into song, missing not a word or a note of a chorus we kids used to sing in children's church:

I'll NEVER let the devil win!
I'll NEVER compromise with him.
He may try me from without,
he may try me from within,
but NEVER will I let the devil win!

I guess his singing caused me to choke up a bit, and he noticed that, too, because when we got home, he took my face in his hands, looked me straight in the eyes and said with all the lucidity in the world, "Look. Everything is going to be OK for you. I believe that. If I didn't believe it, I'd be crying, too." It was as if a bright sun had broken through the clouds in his mind to bring me a message of fatherly love.

While I was living in Phoenix, Mom also came out to visit me at least once a year. And for the most part, those visits were pleasant. She was in her 70s by that time, and we had both mellowed a bit, although our relationship still had quite a way to go. During those visits, I got to see some sides of her that I had never seen before, and she also supplied a missing piece of a puzzle that I had wondered about for more than 30 years.

We were sitting in a Taco Bell having dinner one night when she said in the course of our conversation, "I've been near death many times." This wasn't the first time I had heard her say that, and my reaction was the same as always: Mom is being melodramatic. For most of my life, Mom had been highly energetic and a hard worker between bouts of taking to her bed with a "sick headache," but she also had a habit of complaining about her health in ways that seemed exaggerated. Often, when we were around someone who had a truly serious ailment, I was even embarrassed by her complaints. I thought she was a hypochondriac, looking for attention, and Dad, John and I all tended to ignore her. But now I believe a better response might have been to show her the love she was begging for.

I think Mom's taking on about her health may have been related to her unfulfilled longings for her dad's love. After Mom's death, Aunt Carolyn told me how forlorn Mom had looked standing on the sidewalk with her suitcase when Grandpa had kicked her out at 17. Her relations with her dad had always been rocky—except for when she had been injured as a child. As a preschooler, she was badly burned, she said, when her clothes caught fire from a burning trash pile, and it was her father who had tenderly bandaged and cared for her wounds during her long convalescence. She had no scars that I could see, and she always claimed that she had been healed by her mother's prayers and those of her Aunt Emma, which is why she never lost her faith in God. But I think she also remembered that the only time her dad had been really tender toward her was when she was injured. As we were sitting in the Taco Bell in Phoenix, though, I still didn't understand the connection between her hypochondria and her need for love, so when she said, "I have been near death many times," I challenged her: "When have you ever been near death, Mom? You've never had a major illness or surgery in your life!"

Her response knocked me for a loop.

"When I was 17, I had an abortion and almost died," she said. In all the years since my own abortion and the trouble with the church, she had never talked about any of it. It was if it had never happened. And now, all of a sudden, she was telling me something she had been carrying around for more than 60 years. She wouldn't elaborate or reveal who the father was, dismissing him as "just some guy," so I never found out whether her dad had kicked her out of the house because she was pregnant or whether she had gotten into trouble during that wild couple of years she had lived with her aunt and danced with a beer bucket on her head. She had once said something about having been in love with a man whose letters her mother had destroyed without telling her, so maybe that was the "guy." Maybe he was married—who knows? But at least I finally understood what was behind her statement all those years ago, that she had gone through an experience similar to my own.

During one of Mom's visits, I also learned something I had always suspected about her feelings toward me. Most of the time we enjoyed being together, but occasionally the old differences would flare up, and on one of those occasions she blurted out, "I always thought you came between me and your dad." Sometimes in the past she had said things like, "Your dad and I were very happy before you were born," which made me feel that my birth had changed all that, but she had never told me straight out that she thought I had come between them—until now. And, in some ways, I guess she was right. After all, Dad had declared when I was born that he loved little girls. And I had always been a daddy's girl. When I was very small, people would say, "You look just like your daddy." I had a vague sense even then that she didn't like to hear that. When I was older, Dad and I—and, later, John—sometimes ganged up on her, like the time we had the argument about William Jennings Bryan. So, instead of finally finding someone to love her for herself, maybe she felt she had brought someone into the world who had taken love away from her. But she made another surprising admission during one of those visits to Phoenix. "I was a little crazy when you were growing up," she said.

In Phoenix I also saw another side of Mom. During my lifetime, she had always worn loose clothing and no makeup beyond a little foundation and an imperceptible amount of rouge. She was the antithesis of a sexpot, even if she did have great legs, and graceful, talented hands, but she had told me many times that she had a lot of boyfriends when *she* was young. "I even had three dates in one day!" she declared. I think she said that to encourage me to play the field, but at the time, it felt to me as if she were bragging that she had been more popular than I. She also claimed several times over the years that it was not hard to get a man—that any woman could do it if she knew how. Now, at the age of 75, with half a dozen major love affairs behind me, I understand what she was trying to tell me. I'm a slow learner when it comes to love, so I was a long way from believing her then. But when we first got to Phoenix, she provided a dramatic illustration of what she had been talking about.

I was scheduled to housesit for my new in-laws, who stuck around a few days to get acquainted with Mom before leaving on vacation, and during that time I was utterly flabbergasted to see Mom actually flirt with my father-in-law, a very upright Southern Baptist. He was rather short and spry, and I think he reminded Mom a bit of her brothers. But if I was shocked to see Mom flirt with him, I was even more amazed to see him flirt back. It was all in fun, of course, and if my new mother-in-law was bothered by it, I couldn't tell, but I was certainly seeing a new side to my mom.

Later, on one of Mom's visits after my brief second marriage had ended in divorce, she showed that even though she was in her 70s, she was still attracted to "manly" men. By this time, I had fallen in love with a sprinter who had come to work for American Express in the Olympic Job Opportunities Program. He was young enough to be my son, and he was African-American—two reasons my mother would ordinarily have found more than adequate for objecting to my relationship with him. I didn't tell her I was in love with him, of course, but I realize now that she knew. Mom always knew more about me than I thought, but we both tacitly honored the fiction that he was just a friend. Besides, he was an Olympic gold medalist, he was beautiful, and he could run like the wind. One day when I took Mom to the track to watch him practice, she was entranced. "It's like seeing Mercury come to life!" she declared.

After practice, when he came over to say hello to us, he exerted his usual charm, inviting himself to dinner at my apartment so he could get to know Mom better. "I'll bake you a pie," Mom surprised me by volunteering. But on the morning of the day that he was to come for dinner, she wasn't feeling well and said she didn't think she was up to baking a pie. "That's OK, Mom, I'll bake one," I said, whereupon I could immediately sense that she was not at all happy about that idea. I had to smile to myself when I realized that *she* wanted to be the one to bake a pie for "Mr. Mercury-Come-to-Life."

For the five and a half years I was in Phoenix, Mom had been busy working on *Behold God's Handmaid*, portions of which she would send to me periodically for editing. Between working long hours at American Express and spending several hours a week at the gym to get my body into the kind of shape I erroneously thought it had to be to please "Mr. Mercury-Come-to-Life," I didn't have a lot of spare time, and Mom, never having worked in the corporate world, sometimes got impatient with my tardiness in returning her drafts. In fact, when she finally sent the book off to the printer, she did so without letting me see the galleys, and when the book finally *did* come out, I was distressed to discover that the typography was rather poor and there were still some typos. But before that, something happened that once more changed the course of my life.

One Saturday in the fall of 1988, I called Mom to tell her that I had finally finished editing her book. "You'll be glad to know that I sent your book off to you this morning," I told her.

"What book, Honey?" she asked.

"The book you've been writing for five years," I said.

"I have?" she replied.

I couldn't believe what I was hearing. For the past six or seven years, I had watched my beloved daddy's slow decline into Alzheimer's, first losing his short-term memory, then his ability to read, and, finally, to carry on a conversation. I had seen my stepmother's health suffer as she tried to care for him while keeping life as normal as possible. Once, she had even been hospitalized with pneumonia, probably from the stress that so many

Alzheimer's caretakers experience. Although by this time my job in Phoenix had become more rewarding, both financially and in terms of creative opportunities, I had been thinking for quite awhile that I should quit my job and go back to Illinois to help my stepmother care for Dad, and now, all of a sudden, it sounded as if Mom was going the same route as Dad.

For more than half an hour, my panic intensified as Mom and I talked. She seemed to know nothing about the book she had written, but she kept saying, "There are some books on my table and I don't know where they came from." Periodically, she would interrupt our conversation to go to the front door to see if someone was knocking. My terror during this exchange was indescribable.

And then, suddenly, she was OK.

She knew she had written a book, but she had no memory of our previous half-hour of conversation. That's when I decided that I had to go back to Illinois soon to help care for her and Dad. But I had just turned 50 and I had no savings (I had spent all my previous retirement funds traveling), so I knew I would have to stay at American Express long enough to be vested in the retirement system. Luckily, a law had recently been passed saying that any employee who had worked for a company for at least five years as of January 1, 1989, must be legally vested in its retirement program. Since I had already worked for the company a little more than five years, I figured I had to stay only until sometime past January 1, just three or four months away, to be vested. I went to the benefits officer and told her my plans, and she agreed that if I stayed a couple of weeks into January, I would be vested. Trying unsuccessfully to hold back my tears, I told the senior vice president, Keith Halliday, about Mom's problem and my plans to leave. I had been writing speeches and letters for him for the past couple of years, and when I actually left at the end of January, 1989, he gave me a $3,000 bonus. It was not a usual practice to give someone in my position a parting bonus, I think, so I will always be grateful for his kindness, especially in light of what I had found out about my retirement funds.

In early January, after I had submitted my formal letter of resignation to American Express, I went in to talk to my immediate boss about my severance benefits. She handed me some paperwork, and I was shocked to find that while I had accumulated a bit of American Express stock and some IRAs, the report said "No Retirement Funds." When I protested, she called the benefits office on speakerphone. "Denise, do you remember when you told me I would be vested in the retirement plan if I stayed until sometime in January?" I asked the benefits officer.

"Yes," she replied, "but I called New York, and they said we don't have to be in compliance until December 1."

My heart sank. I knew I couldn't wait another whole year to go back to be with my parents, so even though my boss asked me if I wanted to change my mind, I went ahead with plans to leave at the end of the month. I figured I had a good resume and should be able to find a teaching job with the community college. (When I retired a few years later, it turned out I had been vested for a year or so in the old retirement plan—before IRAs—so today I get approximately $53 a month from American Express, which is fair and legal, I guess, but not what I had hoped for.)

It didn't help, either, that I was leaving behind "Mr. Mercury-Come-to-Life." I had enjoyed some delightful times with him, going out for lunch, attending his presentations to local school children, watching him practice on the track, and talking with him for an hour or more by phone almost every evening. He had a great sense of humor and the most aggressively positive attitude I had ever encountered in my life, so that, even though he was young enough to be my son, I looked up to him in many ways. But I knew that he would soon be moving on without me, whether I left or stayed. The previous summer, I had watched him compete in the Olympic trials in Indianapolis where he missed making his fourth Olympic team by a devastating 1/100 of a second. He had said it would be his last try, after which he intended to move on with his life. The tie between us was deep, but he had never allowed me to harbor any illusions that our relationship, as it was, would last forever. From the beginning, he had explained that, until his Olympic career was over, he was "married to running," after which he would look for a young African American woman to marry. I respected him for his honesty, and we had become good friends, which we are to this day. I left Phoenix with an aching heart but glad, at the same time, to be going back where I might be able to help my parents.

Mom had recovered from what had apparently been a TIA (transient ischemic attack), and she flew out to Phoenix to help me make the drive back to St. Louis. However, she reported that she had experienced one or two more attacks, and I was determined to get some tests done on her to find out what was going on.

One of the first things I did upon arriving in St. Louis in February 1989 was take Mom to Barnes Hospital for a battery of tests. I wanted to find out what had caused her mysterious memory lapses. By then she was 77 years old and taking several medications, so the doctors suggested that side effects or small strokes might have been to blame, but the tests didn't reveal anything definitive. That same year, though, another very troubling incident caused me to worry about Mom's health. While I was still living in the studio apartment, she came over for dinner one evening, after which we were scheduled to go to a concert. At the end of the meal, she said, "Would you look at the back of my head, Pat? I think I may have hit it on something." When I looked, I was shocked to find a large gash on the back of her head and a mass of dried blood in her hair and on her collar. I immediately took her to the hospital, where she received several stitches, but I was puzzled that she had sat all through dinner without mentioning it, and she never could remember how she had incurred the injury.

Two or three years later, she began waking up with blood on her pillow and a mangled tongue, which she had obviously chewed in the night. Things got so bad that she began sleeping with a washcloth tied around her face like a gag, trying unsuccessfully to keep herself from chewing her tongue. Then, one day when I was driving her somewhere, her eyes glazed over and she started chewing away in the middle of our conversation. We had been talking about her plans to drive down to Dallas alone to see my brother and his family, and I had been trying to persuade her to wait, since I thought she was getting too old for such a long drive by herself. I don't know if that was what triggered her attack, but when I yelled at her to stop, she went on staring and chewing, even after I slapped her face, as my dad had done to me so many years before when I had become hysterical. So I drove her straight to the hospital, a mile or so away, and tests revealed that she was having a seizure. Afterwards, she was terribly embarrassed and always insisted that she did "*not* have epilepsy!"

I'm sure part of Mom's concern was a carryover from the days in which epilepsy was a social stigma. In fact, I was in my 20s before I learned from an aunt by marriage that a close member of Mom's family had been suffering from epilepsy for years. No doubt Mom had kept it a secret from me because she assumed, and probably correctly, that I might let the cat out of the bag. I had never been able to understand why some people when I was growing up would whisper the word "cancer," as if there were something shameful about it, or why they would want to hide certain illnesses or conditions like epilepsy. I knew that a lot of famous people, like Julius Caesar, had suffered from epilepsy, and I saw no shame in it, but I suspect some people of my mom's generation might have thought it could be a sign of demon possession, since that primitive belief was still fairly common among fundamentalists. A more practical reason for hiding epilepsy, of course, was that it could prevent sufferers from obtaining certain jobs or a driver's license. But I think maybe the main reason for Mom's resistance to the idea that she had epilepsy was that, for her, it represented a loss of control.

Self-control was always terribly important to Mom—and, indeed, to her whole family, which may be another reason several of them were given to violent outbursts. It takes a lot of effort to stay controlled all the time, and when the pressure builds up to a certain point, the top sometimes blows off. When Grandpa was in the last throes of his congestive heart failure, Mom told me, he had flailed around declaring, "This is something I can't handle!" as if he should have been able to do so. And the family obsession with control was no doubt why Mom never allowed me to squeal like many teenage girls do when excited.

After Mom's attack was diagnosed, I read more about *petit mal* seizures and began to wonder if some of her more erratic behavior over the years might actually have been *petit mal* attacks, since violent temper outbreaks can be one manifestation of the disorder. I remember Dad telling about one time after they had had a particularly savage argument from which he was still feeling depressed, he caught a glimpse of her through the window and was shocked to see her wearing a beatific smile, as if nothing was wrong. He thought it was so strange that he told the story to me two or three times over the years.

When Mom was in her 70s, before I moved from Phoenix to St. Louis, she wrote to me a couple of times about having found herself unconscious on the bathroom floor. Now I realized that those episodes might have been seizures, too. In any case, after she was put on medication, the problem with chewing her tongue stopped, but not without another crisis.

One day when I went to visit her, I was concerned because she seemed extremely lethargic and disoriented. Finally, when she sat down, she pulled up her pants leg and showed me that her leg was dark red, like raw beef. I rushed her to the doctor, who said she was apparently allergic to Dilantin. As when she had cut the back of her head, she had delayed telling me this, introducing the subject almost casually. Although she often took on about what seemed to be imaginary ailments, when she had a *real* injury, she was strangely detached about it. That was one of the things I never did understand about her.

The first couple of years after my return to St. Louis were the most stressful of my life. In addition to worrying about my parents, I lived in a constant state of terror that I would never find another full-time job and would run out of money. When I left Phoenix, I had blithely assumed that, with my resume, I would have no trouble getting a position at a community college in the area, and I was eager to return to teaching, even though it would surely pay less than my position at American Express. But I had neglected to factor in some important details: First, I was 50 years old. Second, I had no way of proving that I had not been fired from the job in Phoenix, since American Express, like many large companies, protected itself from lawsuits by refusing to supply any information about former employees beyond title and dates of employment. Third, I didn't know anyone in St. Louis. And, fourth, the nation was still struggling to get back on its feet from a dramatic 1987 downturn in the stock market.

Having left my furniture in storage in Phoenix until such time as I could find a job in St. Louis, I spent the first eight months sleeping on the floor in a sleeping bag, eating my meals at a card table, watching black-and-white TV, and typing up scores of job application letters on a toy computer, a Coleco-Adam. The TV did double duty as a computer monitor, and the keystroke printer was so loud that you could hear it down the hall, so I put a cardboard box over it to muffle the sound. My only work during that period was teaching an eight-week short course at one of the community college campuses. In the ninth month, I finally found part-time work as a medical editor at $9 an hour, which I supplemented with adjunct teaching at the community college. At the beginning of the semester, I would relax a bit, but as the end grew near, my tension would ramp up again in fear that I would not be called back to work the next semester, and during the first two summers, I had only the part-time editing job to rely on for income.

I still had a $400 a month car note and rent to pay, plus groceries and other normal expenses, and I didn't know how long my money would hold out. I had a prescription for tranquilizers from my days in Phoenix, and I don't remember whether I was able to get a refill in St. Louis, but I know I had some pills left, which I carefully parceled out. Worrying about getting addicted or running out, I would take half a pill or a quarter of a pill, but my nerves were so taut that as I walked down the street, I felt sure people could see my legs and arms jerking spastically, and I had trouble sleeping at night.

One night, I even had a temporary delusion that the city was being invaded by space ships. Without my contacts, I was legally blind, and the prescription for my glasses was way out of date. As I stood looking out my 11th-story picture window, I saw a ring of white lights in the sky and elsewhere, flashing lights of red, green and yellow. I stood looking for a long time, trying to find a logical explanation and finally it dawned on me that if the lights flashed from red to green to yellow to red again, they could be traffic lights. When I eventually concluded that they were, indeed, traffic lights, I decided to go to bed and try not to worry about the ring of white lights. Several days or weeks later, when I was driving down Grand Avenue at night, I realized that what I had thought was a space ship was the ring of lights around the helicopter pad at St. Louis University Hospital. Another night, there was an exceptionally fierce thunderstorm, with lightning bolts seeming to strike all around my building every few minutes. Standing at the picture window, I was convinced that this was the end of the world.

During that time, some quack had also predicted that a major earthquake was going to strike the St. Louis area, and it seemed that all of St. Louis had taken the man seriously. My employers at both the community college and Mosby-Year Book issued bulletins about earthquake preparedness, and the papers were full of accounts of the devastating 1811 earthquake caused by the New Madrid fault, which allegedly caused church bells to ring in Boston and changed the course of the Mississippi River. Lying on the floor in my 11th-story apartment, I imagined the building crumbling and burying me in the rubble, and whenever I drove across the river to visit my mother in Illinois, I was taut with anxiety, expecting to be thrown into the river below at any moment as the bridge collapsed.

Once, in desperation, I called my eldest daughter in Miami, but the only sounds I could get out were weird animal noises. She didn't know what was going on and might have thought that I was drunk, although I have never been drunk in my life. But I've always felt embarrassed about that call and sorry that she had to hear it. I'm sure it must have been disturbing or even frightening to her.

In short, I was having a walking nervous breakdown, but, without health insurance, I couldn't afford to go for medical help or counseling. My condition wasn't improved by a couple of other unfortunate events: While I was still sleeping on the floor, a man was shot and killed down the hall from my door and the murderer was never apprehended. On another occasion, some heavy lumber fell on my thigh at Central Hardware while I was shopping for a piece of plywood to make a desk, leaving me with some permanent nerve damage in that leg for which I did not get adequate care because of my lack of health insurance.

While I was struggling to find full-time work, Harold, who had been married to Christine for several years and was living in Pennsylvania, generously offered to send me a little money each month to help tide me over until I could find a job. I was touched by his gesture but felt I had got myself into that mess and would have to take charge of getting myself out. Instead of accepting his help, I opted to live on my IRAs and stock until I could get on my feet again. I did accept a small loan from my mother once or twice, which I paid back within a week or two. And as has happened so many times in my life, there seemed to be an unseen hand guiding events, because just as I spent the last IRA paying the taxes on the previous ones that I had cashed in to live on, I found a position as a planning coordinator at Harris-Stowe State College, the Historically Black College where I would work for most of the rest of my career. The job was only 60 percent time to start, but it came with benefits, and I was able to supplement my income from that job with adjunct teaching at the community college.

Although I had moved back to the area to be near my parents, I had opted to live in St. Louis, rather than on the Illinois side of the Mississippi, where they both lived, because I had fond memories of trips to the city as a child and young adult, and I had often thought I would like to live in the big city. Besides, aware of my mother's strong hold over me, I didn't want to live too close to her. So I had rented a studio apartment on Lindell Blvd. in the Central West End of St. Louis. Midway between St. Louis University and Washington University, the Central West End is a neighborhood of beautiful old homes, apartment buildings, trendy restaurants, art galleries, shops and hotels about a 30-minute drive from Belleville, Illinois, where Mom was living, and a little closer to Dad's, in Fairview Heights. Whenever Mom visited me, she would always say, "I sure wouldn't want to live in St. Louis!" and once she said, "When you and John were growing up, your dad wanted us to move over to this neighborhood, but I thought it was no place to raise children." I was secretly pleased to learn that, without knowing it, I had come straight as a homing pigeon to the St. Louis neighborhood my dad had loved. It was that old ESP thing again.

And despite my high level of anxiety, I enjoyed a lot of things about living in St. Louis. I had a beautiful view of the St. Louis Cathedral out my 11th-story window and I loved exploring the city while waiting for responses to my job applications. I often walked a few blocks down Lindell Boulevard to the Hari Krishna restaurant, Govinda's, where the food was cheap and nutritious and where Govinda, a Catholic convert to the Krishna movement, assured me that everything was going as it should, that all my needs were being met—as, in fact, they were. I bought cheap groceries at Aldi's and second-hand clothing and kitchen utensils in the Goodwill.

I was able to pay my bills without going into debt, and my credit rating remained good. If I hadn't been plagued by anxiety, it could have been a delightful period of R&R after my five-and-a-half busy years of working at American Express. Looking back later on, I realized that FDR's statement that "the only thing we have to fear is fear itself" was certainly true of me during that time.

Despite all these problems, though, I never regretted returning to St. Louis when I did, because it allowed me to spend some precious time with my dad during the last months of his life. During that first year, my stepmother often brought Dad over to spend Sundays with me while she went to church in St. Louis County. I had joined the First Unitarian Church of St. Louis, the same church at which Dad had made his short break for religious freedom in the 1960s, and I thought he would enjoy going back. So I invited him to walk there with me one Sunday, but I didn't realize how weak he had become. Although the church was only half a dozen blocks away, he had to sit down and catch his breath several times. During the coffee hour after church, one of the members introduced himself to Dad, and when I told him Dad had briefly attended there in the 1960s, the man asked if Dad remembered some person from those days. "I don't believe I do," he said, getting out one of the longer sentences he was able to put together at the time and perhaps preventing the man from realizing that he was suffering from Alzheimer's. After that Sunday, we stayed at home, where he would gaze out the window, enjoying the view, while I fixed lunch for him and tried to make conversation. For a good part of the time, he would stretch out on the floor and take a nap. Unlike some Alzheimer's sufferers, he never became irritable or angry, even when he lost the ability to carry on a conversation or figure out exactly where he was, so the time I had with him was precious, especially since it turned out to be so short.

I don't remember the details of how this came about, but one time during those first few months back in St. Louis, I also took Dad by to see Mom at her apartment in Belleville. I felt a little guilty about it, since I hadn't told my stepmother what I was doing. In fact, I'm not even sure I knew I was going to do it until the impulse hit me. But Dad and I were out for a drive, and I just decided to stop by Mom's apartment and see if she was home. I knew I wouldn't be encouraging a secret liaison because both of them were too old for that sort of thing, and Dad was too far gone with his disease, but I guess I just wanted to see them together one more time. We didn't go in, but Mom came out to the car and Dad got out and stood beside her. The memory of seeing them standing together, smiling, with their arms around each other, still touches my heart.

On Saturdays, I also made frequent trips across the river to take Mom out to dinner and play Scrabble with her, but I resisted the temptation to spend the night. Often, during Saturday afternoons, though, we took little drives around the area to explore the countryside. On July 4, 1989, just five months after my arrival in St. Louis, we drove up to Alton, Illinois, to visit one of Mom's many cousins, and when we arrived back at Mom's house in the late afternoon, we found a note on the front porch saying, "Call your Aunt Elsie." Elsie was Uncle Jim's wife and one of my favorite people, so I wasn't particularly disturbed to see the message, thinking maybe she wanted us to come over for supper. But when I called, she had devastating news: "Your dad's gone," she said.

My stepmother had taken excellent care of Dad as his illness worsened, and the two of them were still in the habit of traveling quite a bit to visit her two sons, who were working on opposite coasts. They had just returned from one of those trips, I learned, when Dad sat down on the couch and died without warning. During his long illness, I had sometimes thought that if I could get away with it, I would be tempted to put him out of his misery, but when I went to the hospital and saw his cold, stiff form lying on a gurney in a side room, I knew that I never could have done it. What I saw there was a chrysalis; my beloved daddy was indeed gone, and a part of me went with him.

It wasn't until several months later, though, after a special service at church to commemorate the loss of friends and family members who had died during the past year that I broke down completely. When I got home, I sobbed my heart out in my room alone. A young African-American man whom I barely knew, living in the apartment next door, must have heard me, because for the rest of the time I lived there he was especially solicitous, sending me cards on special occasions and once giving me some flowers. Although I was and still am an agnostic, there were several incidents in my life like that which I choose to call "the hand of God," since they offered comfort, seemingly out of nowhere, when I needed it the most.

There were two memorial services for Dad: one in the little church in St. Louis County which he and my stepmother had attended for several years, and one in the SIUE library, for which he had worked for 19 years. During the service at the church, the minister said he had never known Dad before his illness, but he'd heard that Dad was a a good speaker and a man who loved to read, so it must have been hard for him to lose his ability to express himself. When the minister finished speaking, two people in the congregation—one the mother of a disabled child and the other a young African-American woman—volunteered that Dad had still been able to convey a message of love, offering a smile and tender pats whenever he saw them.

Many people from all walks of life came to honor Dad at the service in the library, including distinguished professors, co-workers, and people he had met both as a preacher and a book collector. Two collections of Americana were established in his name: one at the Lovejoy Library of SIUE and another one at the Mercantile Library on the campus of the University of Missouri-St. Louis. Harold came from Pennsylvania for the service in the library and read such a moving tribute to Dad that when it was my turn to read, I could barely hold back my tears.

Mom also came to that service, sitting in the back and leaving as soon as it was over. When I stopped by her house later that day, I found her alone in the dusk, playing the piano with no lights on.

After Dad's death, Mom and I spent even more time together. At first I resisted staying overnight at her house, but I gradually fell into a pattern of going over on Saturday evening, after I had finished my shopping and household chores, to take her to dinner. After dinner, we would go to her house and play Scrabble for the rest of the evening. During the first year or two, I usually went home after Scrabble, but when Mom moved to an assisted living facility, and as my vision deteriorated to the point that I didn't feel safe driving home in the dark, I began staying overnight. Soon I was going with her to church on Sunday morning and taking her out to lunch before returning to my condo in St. Louis.

By then, I had found a good job and fallen in love again—this time with a man who, I was convinced, could help restore many of the things I had enjoyed so much about marriage and family life. The chemistry between us was immediate and powerful. What's more, he had all the necessary qualifications: Just two years younger than I, he was well-educated, good-looking, wealthy, charming and unmarried. He even had a daughter who was an attorney, and since I now had two daughters who were attorneys, I immediately conjured up an elaborate fantasy of a blended family in which we would all come together for holidays in his stately St. Louis mansion and he and I would live happily ever after.

There were, however, a couple of problems: He was chairman of the board of the college where I had eventually found full-time work. Our positions, he said, made it impossible for us to date publicly. The second problem, which he hadn't bothered to mention, was that he was a playboy who had a much younger, very beautiful public girlfriend (as well as others on the side, so the rumors went) and he had no intention of marrying me. To his credit, he had warned me from the beginning about becoming "too possessive," but like many a woman blinded by love, I heard only what I wanted to hear. I didn't learn about the younger girlfriend until I was too deeply mired in my own fantasy to give it up. Already in my middle 50s, I saw "The Chairman" as my last chance for domestic bliss, and the vision I had created was so compelling that I was unable to let go of it—or him—for many years. The only really positive side of this situation was that he spent his weekends out of town or with his young girlfriend, so I was able to spend mine with Mom, and during those years we continued to grow closer. Sometimes she would say "I love you"—words that I had longed for so many years to hear—and give me a kiss.

For several reasons, I didn't tell Mom about my new love—the main one being that the affair was clandestine, and I knew she would not approve or might even assume that he was married, even if I told her otherwise. "Don't ever take another woman's husband," she had often cautioned me. But one evening when I arrived at her place shortly after I had experienced a very disturbing session with The Chairman, she sensed that I was upset and asked me what was the matter. Although I had always felt uncomfortable about sharing my deepest feelings with her—I was afraid she might use the knowledge to hurt me—this time I couldn't contain my emotion. Breaking into tears, I told her what was going on, and her response was uncharacteristically nonjudgmental and strangely comforting: "Well, I can see that you're in a very tough situation" she said, "and I'm sorry to hear it."

And that was it.

From time to time over the next few years, she would notice I had some expensive new trinket that I obviously couldn't afford, and I could tell she guessed where it had come from, but she never said anything about the subject again. I appreciated her restraint. After her death, I learned that she had shared some concerns about my relationships with her siblings, but, being a mother myself, I could understand that and didn't hold it against her.

During the last years of her life, I came to realize that Mom really did love me, despite how difficult she could be at times, and I developed some strategies for coping with the times that were hardest for me. Before she got really infirm, she would occasionally write a letter to me, even though we lived only half an hour apart and saw each other almost every weekend. Remembering the letter in which she had said, "I am NOT your friend," and aware of the family tradition of poison pen letters, I always read the return address with fear and trembling. I didn't want to risk resurrecting the painful feelings that had caused problems between us in the past. So I forced myself to throw away Mom's letters without reading them. This was hard to do, because I am a document hoarder. I have letters in my study right now from members of my family going back to forever, including Mom's letters from age seventeen on to *her* mother.

The next time I saw her, I would act as if nothing had changed, and she would never mention her recent letter; we just went on as before. I knew there was a possibility that she thought she had really "taught me a lesson" and that I was "shaping up," but I no longer felt I was in a contest with my mother that I had to win. I just wanted us to be happy together. I also knew there was a possibility that she had written something incredibly revealing or wonderfully sweet that I had thrown away without reading. I will never know, but I know that we loved each other, and that's what matters most. In the last year of her life, on the rare occasions when she became a bit crotchety, I would simply lean down and give her a hug or silently press my forehead against hers, and things were all right again.

Of course things didn't always go smoothly between us, but we had a lot of good times during the last fourteen years I spent with Mom, and I was grateful for them. I took her on several road trips, including one to Electra, Texas, where the church was having a homecoming for all the former pastors and members, and another to Paducah, Kentucky, to try to find the tobacco barn in which Mom had been pastoring a church in a rented room when she met Dad. In Electra, someone made a video of

Mom singing and playing the piano, which I cherish. In Paducah, Mom wasn't able to locate the building where her church had met, but she told me about how she had boarded with a family there in an old warehouse along the riverfront and how she could hear the water lapping up below the floorboards.

On Saturday afternoons back in Illinois, we often drove around the countryside, looking for new places to have lunch or dinner, and on Sundays we attended church at Bethel Tabernacle, which had relocated from East St. Louis to a lovely new building in Shiloh, Illinois. The pastor was the same one who had come when Mom and Dad gave up the church in the 1950s some 40 years earlier, but the congregation was extremely small, sometimes no more than a dozen people. There were still a couple of families who had supported us during the vote of confidence, and Mom occasionally was asked to sing and play for services. One Sunday when we were sitting talking in the car outside the church after the service, I mentioned "the time when our church broke up."

"When was that?" Mom asked. "I don't think I remember it." When I reminded her, she knew immediately, but I was amazed that an incident which had exerted such a major impact on my life and my psyche—one I had played and replayed in my mind with varying levels of guilt and regret for a lifetime—now had so little significance in my mother's memory. Still, I believe it had a huge impact on the course of her life, as well as my dad's and even my brother's, whether or not they recognized it. I guess it's all a matter of perspective.

During this period, Mom was still selling *Behold God's Handmaid* by sending out letters and brochures to women across the U.S., and the book was still being carried by the Gospel Publishing House. I'm sure it was enormously gratifying to her to know that, even though the Assemblies of God had deprived her of her papers more than a decade earlier, she had an audience, and the denomination's publishing house was helping her to reach it. A couple of other things happened, too, that gave her a delicious feeling of vindication, I suspect.

I always thought Mom's conception of God derived more from the Old Testament than from The Sermon on the Mount: In her view, it seemed, a major part of God's role was to smite her enemies, so when she believed that someone had done her wrong, she was quick to pounce on evidence suggesting they had received their just desserts. This was obvious when she learned that the presbyter who had advised her, years earlier, to take to her rocking chair and let the younger men of the church take over had begun to experience, himself, some of the indignities of old age. No longer a presbyter or pastor of a large church, he had recently moved to a nearby community where he was rumored to be assuming a lesser position as assistant or interim pastor of a small congregation—I am sketchy on the details. What I do know for sure is that Mom bought a cute miniature rocking chair in the Cracker Barrel restaurant where I often took her for dinner on Saturday nights and she struggled with her conscience for a long time about sending it to the former presbyter with a friendly little note about taking to his rocking chair.

Her good angel won out that time, but it had a harder time when Dick Dortch, her former friend and the presbyter who had taken away her ordination as an Assemblies of God minister, had the gall to send her an autographed copy of his book, along with a letter informing her that it was time for her to forgive him. In the years since that traumatic event in Mom's life, the Rev. Dortch had experienced a bit a trauma of his own. In his case, the details had been plastered all over the national headlines. As president of televangelist Jim Bakker's PTL Club, he had engaged in some financial skullduggery for which, in 1988, he and some of his fellow PTL buddies were indicted on federal charges of fraud and conspiracy. Taking a plea bargain, he had received a reduced sentence of eight years in prison, which was later cut to two-and-a-half years. But like a lot of high-profile people who go to prison, Richard Dortch had been able to spin straw into gold by writing several books about his experience. The one he sent Mom, ironically entitled *Fatal Conceit: A Bold Challenge to Everyone in This Power-Hungry World*, was inscribed, "To my friend Mary Ruth Chamless.

May God's very best be yours. You are loved!" It was accompanied by a letter in which he informed her that it was time for her to forgive him. He had forgiven the reporter who had broken the story, he said, and the prosecutor who had sent him to prison, so she should forgive him. And, besides, he had done the right thing in taking away her papers, he added.

I wasn't present when Mom received these peace offerings, but I can testify that she seemed distinctly unmoved when she told me about them, and I know she never responded to his request for "forgiveness." After Dortch's release from prison, the presbyters had restored his accreditation in 1991 and, according to Wikipedia, "Until just prior to his death he hosted a long-standing two- to three-hours prayer service called 'America's Prayer Meeting' on the Christian Television Network. The nightly broadcast reached 55 million households around the world."

In my imagination I can hear Mom muttering an unladylike expletive—the one she had shocked me with in those long-ago arguments with Dad when I was growing up.

From time to time over the years, I thought about what had happened in my teens, especially when my birthday rolled around. One time in my early thirties I realized that I had made it halfway through a birthday without thinking about the abortion or counting up how old the child would be. On that day, Harold and I had been celebrating my birthday by taking a weekend motor trip through southern Ohio—just the two of us—ambling along with no destination in mind and picnicking at roadside tables. I remember the trip as one of the best experiences of our life together.

Throughout my life, I had also periodically thought about Ronnie, wondering how things had turned out for him. A mutual acquaintance, I don't remember who, had told me he owned a service station in the Metro-East area of St. Louis, but when I returned to St. Louis in 1989, I didn't try to find it. But I couldn't resist looking him up in the phone book, and once I actually called his home. "He ain't here," a young male voice answered, whereupon I thanked him and hung up without leaving a name or message. The occasion on which I finally did see him again was one that I could not have imagined in my wildest fantasies.

When Mom was in her 80s, she was hospitalized several times for various ailments, most of which the hospital was unable to do anything about. During one of her stays at Belleville Memorial Hospital, Mom was lying half-asleep as I sat quietly by her bed in the darkened room when a middle-aged, balding man of medium height, wearing glasses, walked in and announced, "I'm the Reverend Ronald C____."

I didn't know what to say. It was the name of my long-lost love, but this man neither looked nor sounded like the boy I had run away to marry at 14. Besides, that boy hadn't been especially religious—he had only come to church to satisfy his mom and, later, to see me. What's more, he had dropped out of school as soon as possible. So it was highly unlikely that this man in front of me was my old love.

"I used to know someone by that name, but you're clearly not he," I said with a casual air that I hoped gave no hint of the startling effect of his announcement.

"Oh, I don't know—depends on how far back you go," he said.

"At least 40 years," I said.

His next words really knocked the wind out of me:

"Bethel Tabernacle?"

"You're *that* Ronald?"

"Yep."

"Do you know who I am?"

"No."

"I'm Pat."

I think that's when he sat down in the chair beside me. If he was experiencing anything like the emotions that were flooding my system, it's a wonder either of us could even speak.

I can't remember our exact words after that. I was too busy trying to figure out how the tall, dark, and handsome boy I had loved—the boy who had been with me at the center of a controversy that had changed all our lives—could be the dignified middle-aged man in the chair next to mine. And I was stunned to think that the former sweetheart who had been so angry with me—and my parents—was this man who had suddenly appeared in my mother's hospital room to pray for her.

I don't remember what I told him about myself—just the basics, I guess, that I was divorced and had three grown daughters, and that I had lived in other states for 20 years and had worked first as a teacher and later as a writer/editor. I don't remember everything he told me, either, but I learned that he was married, had four grown children, and that his family liked to travel across the U.S. in their recreational vehicle. He had been in the construction business, he said, and several years earlier he had taken a bad fall, in which he had broken his back. For more than a year he had lain in bed, unable to walk. The doctors had replaced some of the broken bones in his back with cadaver bones, which may explain why he seemed considerably shorter than I remembered.

While he was bedridden, he said, some people from the congregation of the well-known televangelist Joyce Meyers had come to pray for him, and he had been healed. He had given his heart to God and joined her church. Sometime thereafter, he discovered that he had "a healing ministry," which was authenticated by the church. So now he was spending his time going to hospitals, nursing homes and other places, praying for the sick. He had been to India, he told me, and was getting ready to go to Israel. Or maybe he said he had been to Israel and was getting ready to go to India. I was too stunned to take it all in. We never mentioned what had happened so long ago.

During all this, Mom lay quietly, as if asleep, and after awhile Ronnie stood, laid his hands on her head, and said a prayer for her. I don't think they exchanged any words, and I don't remember how we said goodbye. That night I went home and wrote in my journal, "The most amazing thing that has ever happened to me happened tonight . . ."

I saw Ronnie only one more time, but that would not be the end of our story. In the meantime, I learned some more startling information. My Uncle Jim, Mom's brother to whose home Faye and I had fled all those years before with Ronnie's Pontiac in hot pursuit, was now a good friend of my former sweetheart. After the death of my Aunt Elsie a few years earlier, Uncle Jim had married a woman named Bonnie, and sometime after their marriage she had become a member of the church where Ronnie now had a healing ministry. I didn't know Bonnie when Jim married her, and I'm sure she didn't know anything about all that had gone on at Bethel Tabernacle in the 1950s—she might not have even been born yet, as she was much younger than my uncle—but she had met Ronnie at the church and liked him, so she invited him and his wife home for dinner. I don't know if the two men instantly recognized each other from their long-ago encounter, but they quickly became friends, something I gathered Uncle Jim had avoided telling Mom before Ronnie showed up in her hospital room. "He's a really sweet guy," Uncle Jim told me later. So perhaps Jim had told Ronnie that Mom was in the hospital and Ronnie had come there on purpose to pray for his old nemesis. Or perhaps it was an accident. I will never know.

After Ronnie's dramatic appearance in the hospital, Uncle Jim provided another example of the strange coincidences that have cropped up with disturbing regularity throughout my life. Ronnie had been involved somehow in the construction of the famous Gateway Memorial Arch on the St. Louis riverfront, Uncle Jim said. Somewhat afraid of heights and even more afraid of tightly enclosed spaces, I have never been able to screw up my courage to ride to the top of the Arch in those little cars, which remind me of egg cartons, but I am so fascinated by that amazing structure and the brave men who had worked on it that I have watched the movie about its construction at least four times. "I would run away with any man who worked on the Arch!" I used to laughingly declare to friends. As it turned out, apparently I *had* run away with one of them.

A week or so after Mom got out of the hospital, when I went over to visit her in the assisted living facility, she said, "Your boyfriend was here."

"What boyfriend?" I asked, truly puzzled.

"Ronnie," she said. "I think he was looking for you."

I don't know whether he actually came to Mom's apartment or whether she had imagined it. She had been having some hallucinations of late, telling me on several occasions that a little boy had come inside her patio door and stood beside her bed, so I assumed this was another hallucination. Her comment did suggest, however, that although she had not appeared to recognize Ronnie in the hospital, it's possible that she had heard our whole conversation. I never made any attempt to see if Ronnie had actually tried to contact me. What could I say, after all this time? But I was happy to know that his life had turned out so well.

I did see Ronnie one more time a few months later when I went to visit Uncle Jim, who was a patient in the same hospital where Mom had been. Ronnie was there, along with his wife, whom he introduced. I was so flustered that I can't remember anything about her, except that she seemed like a very nice person. As was my custom, though, I tried to appear at ease and in control.

Eventually, the time came when I had to put Mom in a nursing home in St. Louis—two places she had never wanted to be. I felt bad about it, but she needed constant care, and I could not afford to stop working before I was eligible for retirement from my job at the college, so I put her in a very nice place only five minutes from the college and about the same distance from my condo. When she went in, I was not expecting her to live more than a few days, but she surprised me by living another year and a half, and she even regained enough function to be able to carry on a conversation and get around in a wheelchair. I visited her almost daily, often stopping by a fast food place at lunchtime to get some sandwiches we could share while sitting on one of the balcony sun porches.

Those were sweet days, in which she was very solicitous of my welfare, wanting to know where I lived and who lived with me. When she found out that I lived alone, she surprised me by asking, "Do you have much intercourse?" Since my romance with The Chairman had gone into hibernation at that point, I had to admit, "No, not much, Mom," but I was touched by her concern and amused by her candor.

During our meals together, Mom usually tried to share her food with me, and I would have to point out that I had food of my own, but she would soon forget and offer me a bite of her sandwich again. Sometimes on Saturday nights, I would take her and her wheelchair to Steak 'n Shake for dinner, and once I saw The Chairman there with another woman—a white woman who was not his public fiancée. As usual, I tried to appear calm and friendly, stopping by his booth to say hello and introducing my mother, although I doubt that she made the connection with the man in my earlier confession.

Mom never let on that she knew she was in a nursing home in St. Louis, and she often didn't seem to know where we were going when we took a ride, but once she remarked as we drove up Magnolia Avenue by Tower Grove Park, "I enjoy these little outings." And sometimes when we came back to the nursing home afterwards, she was reluctant to get out of the car. One night when she was being especially stubborn about it, I said, "Mama, you can't sit here all night," whereupon she set her little chin in a hard line and, staring straight ahead, replied, "I'll bet I can!" That was my mama—determined to the end, and by this time I found her behavior rather endearing.

We had Mom's 90th birthday party in the elegant dining room of the historic Civil War mansion attached to her nursing home. Uncle Jim, Uncle Bob, and a couple of members from Bethel Tabernacle in the old days were among the guests. By her 91st birthday, on January 29, 2003, she was more confused, and the celebration was less elaborate, but still there were flowers, balloons, and cards from friends.

By that time, Mom had been in hospice care for several months, and early in the morning on April 19, 2003, someone from Beauvais Manor called to tell me she was failing. When I walked into her room to find her hooked up to oxygen, I grabbed her hand and she held onto it without opening her eyes or speaking a word. After awhile, when I crawled into bed with her, she pulled the oxygen tube out of her nose. When I put it back, she pulled it out again and, knowing that she had signed a living will, I said, "OK, Mom, if you don't want it, you don't have to have it." Holding her in my arms, I tearfully asked her to forgive me for all the times I had hurt or misunderstood her.

It's hard for me to believe, even now, that I fell asleep while my mother was dying, but I did. When I woke, she was still breathing lightly, but a few minutes later, she gave a big sigh and it was all over. Going out to the desk, I told the nurse, "My mother is gone," and then I fell into the arms of a nearby African-American male attendant who patiently held me while

I sobbed. I have often reflected since that day that, in the end, Mom got what she had always wanted. All her life she had longed for somebody to love her just for herself, and that person turned out to be me.

As it happened, Mom died just a month before I was able to retire from my job at the college. For the previous five months, I had been desperately hoping to take her to live with me in Stillwater, Oklahoma, near two of my daughters and closer to my brother and his family in Dallas. In fact, just a week before her death I had signed the papers on a darling hundred-year-old house in Stillwater with a huge yard, and porches on three sides, one of which even had an old-fashioned swing. I had visions of Mom sitting out on the east-facing porch enjoying the sunshine and visits from her grandchildren and son, but that was not to be. Although she was "out of it" a lot of the time during the last months of her life, she told one of the nurses that we were going to move, so she was aware that I had been looking for a house near the girls and John.

Arriving back at the nursing home on my way home from signing the papers for the house, I had told her, "Mom, I bought the house!" "You bought the house?" she said. "Good." That was only a few days before she died. I will always believe she decided then that it was OK for her to die because I would be back near my family and no longer alone.

Without Mom, the move to Stillwater was bittersweet, but it turned out to be one of the best periods in my life since my divorce from Harold. Having been so profligate with my retirement funds over the years, I had never expected to own a home after retirement, but several unexpected developments helped me find the resources. Mom's brother Bill, married with no children, had died a few years after my move to St. Louis and left all six of his surviving siblings a generous bequest. On two or three occasions, Mom had given some of that money to my brother and me, which was a big help when I was trying to regain my financial footing after the years in which I had spent all my retirement funds trying to find a job. By the time of Mom's death, most of her inheritance from Uncle Bill had gone to the nursing home, but the small amount I received from her estate, combined with my profit from the sale of my condo in St. Louis, enabled me to pay off my credit cards and car note and make a down payment on the little house in Stillwater.

It was pure heaven to have a home and large yard of my own, with an abundance of tall trees and a long, east-facing porch on which I could enjoy breakfast while reading a book, or rock slowly in the porch swing while listening to the chimes from nearby Oklahoma State University, where I had been a freshman almost half a century earlier. Lying upstairs in the tiny bedroom under the eaves, I was transported back to the upstairs bedroom of my childhood in Collinsville, and, at other times, to the attic bedroom in Dayton, where my daughters had spent some of their teen years. Now living a little over an hour's drive from my youngest daughter, an attorney in Enid, and my eldest, a law professor in Tulsa, I got to see them more often than I had done since they had gone away to college.

John and his family were in Dallas, only about six hours' drive away, so I also visited them several times and was delighted to receive a visit from John's two children, Paul and Patricia, who were young enough to be my grandchildren. If my middle daughter, a philosophy professor in Philadelphia, had not lived so far away, things would have been perfect. In Stillwater I came as close as I had ever done to recreating the family life I had missed for so many years since my divorce from Harold. The first summer after my move, in fact, I hosted a family reunion to which the girls and their spouses; John and his wife, Kathryn; and Harold and his wife, Christine, all came for a weekend. It was a great feeling having everyone together again.

A bonus in the move to Stillwater was that my neighbors were exceptionally kind, as were the many friends I made over the next five years. I joined the Weekly Meeting of Quakers in Stillwater and went to work on my "bucket list" by teaching composition part-time at Oklahoma State University and Northern Oklahoma College and, for two years, writing a column in the *Stillwater News Press*. For a brief stint, I even served as a reporter there, but staying up until 2 a.m. to meet deadlines became too much for me. My time in Oklahoma was a blessed interlude for which I will always be grateful. Although I moved back to an apartment in St. Louis when I realized that the house would eventually bankrupt me, both physically and financially, I still make frequent visits to all the dear people who befriended me there.

While I was living in Stillwater, I had another amazing revelation about that long-ago incident that had colored so much of my life. In the summer of 2004, I took a leisurely drive out west to visit several friends and relatives, and on this trip I visited Uncle Wes and his wife, Louise, who were living in the Phoenix area. One day when Aunt Louise was out of the house, Uncle Wes startled me by asking, "Pat, do you remember what happened to you when you were 15?"

I had always thought no one in Dad's family knew about my pregnancy, so I was startled by the question. "Yes," I answered cautiously.

"Did you know that your dad asked us if you could stay with us and have the baby?" he said.

This was the first I had heard of such a thing, and I have pondered the possibilities ever since. I had always assumed that Mom took the lead in setting up the abortion—after all, her brother Bill had lent her the money and most likely had put her in touch with the doctors and the attorney—but it had never occurred to me that Dad had been considering other options. And although I believed the abortion had been Mom's decision, I had never blamed her for it, especially after I became a mother myself. In those days, pregnant girls did not attend high school, unwed mothers were an embarrassment to everyone, and children born out of wedlock were still considered "bastards," so the choices seemed to be marriage, abortion, or having the child and giving it up for adoption.

I could see why Mom would not want her daughter to become a high-school dropout and housewife at 15, let alone a mother. And I had always thought that having an abortion, while admittedly traumatic, was less so than having a baby and giving it away. I was sure I would never have rested, not knowing what had happened to my baby and whether it was having a good life. But if Uncle Wes and Aunt Louise had raised the baby as their own, I would have known where the child was and could have visited, and I probably could have re-entered high school after a year's "illness." Wes and Louise never had a child of their own, so perhaps it would have brought joy to their life. Or not. Of course that scenario completely ignores the fact that the baby would have been Ronnie's as well, and he surely would have wanted some say in the matter.

I often remember a daydream I had when I was around 12 years old in which I imagined that I would one day be the mother of four beautiful and talented daughters, and people would say, "There goes Pat, the mother of those four beautiful daughters!" Recalling that daydream, I have sometimes wondered if the baby I never had could have been that fourth daughter. But then I tell myself that if I had married Ronnie and had his baby, I would never have borne the three wonderful daughters I have now. On the other hand, if I had given the baby up to Uncle Wes and Aunt Louise, I might still have married Harold and had my three present-day daughters, plus a fourth. But our lives go only one way, and we can only speculate about what might have been.

A couple of years after my move to Stillwater, Uncle Jim called to tell me that Ronnie had died from a heart attack while on vacation in Florida. The obituary listed him as a pastoral assistant whose mission was to visit people in hospitals and nursing homes "wherever the Lord called him." He was described by one of his sons as a loving father who always had time for his children despite a busy work schedule, a person on whom others could depend in an emergency, and someone who lived life to the fullest, going on 4-wheel jamborees and bike tours and traveling in his RV. "As the end of his life drew near, he was the happiest he had ever been," his son wrote.

My hands still retain the tactile memory of my young lover's head, and after more than 60 years I can still hear his voice saying, "Let's go, Jackson!" when we went for rides in his Pontiac with Richard driving, but it was almost impossible for me to detect any resemblance between the boy I remembered and the man I had met in the hospital or now saw in the obituary photo. Still, I was grateful that, somehow, we had managed to meet once more in a friendly way before he departed from this earth.

I also wondered how Mom would feel if she could have known what kind of man her almost son-in-law turned out to be. I couldn't help noticing the irony that the man I eventually married—and who fathered her grandchildren—was an atheist, while the boy she had prevented me from marrying turned out to be a minister, like herself.

It would be over-romanticizing my story to suggest that my life would have been happier if I had married Ronnie. Our interests and personalities were too different. I think Harold Piety was the right man to father my children, and if I had been less insecure and immature, perhaps the right man to spend my life with. But he found a good wife, and I was glad of that. As for Ronnie, it seems obvious that the woman he married, and with whom he apparently had a happy family, was the right woman for him. And despite the rather roller-coaster trajectory of my own life, it has been full of love and packed with adventure. What's more, I honestly believe that every bad experience I've had and every mistake I've made has taught me something about how to love, appreciate, and empathize with my fellow human beings—how to see the other side of things—although I still have a long way to go in that regard.

In my declining years, my physical passions and romantic fantasies have subsided to a more manageable level, so that I am reasonably content—most of the time. All my life I've been impatient, and for much of it I've been plagued by depression or anxiety, so being reasonably content most of the time is progress. My three daughters are all socially responsible, loving and successful professionals: Tamara R. Piety is a law professor at the University of Tulsa and author of a book called *Brandishing the First Amendment*, about corporate use of First Amendment free speech rights. Marilyn (M.G.) Piety is a philosophy professor at Drexel University who has authored three books—one, published by Oxford University Press, is a translation from the Danish of two works by Danish philosopher Søren Kierkegaard. And Julia Rieman is a gifted attorney, licensed to argue before the U.S. Supreme Court, whose many successful appeals are frequently cited by attorneys in other cases.

I'm grateful for a lot of things: those last, sweet years with my parents, a loving circle of friends, a life full of variety, and my two adorable cats, Daisy and Felix, who provide an ever-ready antidote to loneliness. I'm also pleased to have maintained a warm and rewarding relationship with Harold and Christine, his wife of more than 30 years.

Harold is in his 80s as I write this, and he is still in good health, which is indeed a blessing. For Thanksgiving 2012, he baked a turkey with all the trimmings and five kinds of pies for 17 people, including our three daughters, Christine's children and grandchildren, assorted in-laws, friends—and me. Feeling Father Time breathing down all our necks, I had invited myself to this traditional meal at their home in Pennsylvania, and Harold and Christine, along with her two children, made me feel very welcome. At the end of the meal, Harold announced that because he was getting too old for the labor involved in such extravaganzas, this would be the last time he would undertake to host one. So I was especially glad that I had come.

While I have a good deal of contentment in my present life and even look forward to the possibility of more adventures before the last great adventure of departing this earth, the past will always remain a vital part of the whole for me.

In the process of writing this book, I went through a lot of old papers, throwing away the ones that no longer seemed useful or relevant, and for a week or two the floor was cluttered with stuff I had yet to sort out. One day, I looked down and saw one of my daughter Tamara's cards from her stint as a teaching fellow at Stanford law school, and I noticed there was another business card beneath it. When I pulled it out, this is what I found:

> **RON C**
> *He sent His word and healed them.*
> *Psalm 107:20*
>
> **Home**   **Pager**
> 618·   321

I didn't recall having received this card from Ronnie, so it seemed almost like a message from The Beyond. A few days later, I had a dream about him. In my dream, I called him up, and he was surprised to hear from me.

"I'm not trying to have an affair with you or break up your marriage," I said in my dream, "it's just that we have old ties, and I'd like to talk."

"That's dangerous," he said.

"Do you think so?"

"Painful," he said.

"Yes, it is that," I conceded.

I thought I heard tears in his voice.

"Please don't be sad," I said. "I love you."

In the background, I could hear his wife asking, "Who is it?"

Afterword About My Brother

I haven't said much about my brother in all this because his childhood was very different from mine, and his memories of our parents, which correspond with mine in some ways, diverge somewhat in others. He wasn't alive, of course, during those years that Mom and Dad were on the road or working for the Bible college in Waxahachie, and he was only seven years old when Bethel Tabernacle broke up, so he never experienced a total immersion in the closed religious lifestyle that I did. In fact, he confessed to me recently that he had never read our mother's book, *Behold God's Handmaid*. "I just don't have any interest in that stuff," he said.

He was nine years old when I went off to college and not yet eleven when I married Harold, who was a combination big brother/second father to him, so it's not too surprising that he graduated from the University of Illinois, like Harold, and became a journalist, also like Harold.

When I think about the ways all of our lives might have been different if I had married Ronnie and become a mother at fifteen, or if the church had never broken up over the scandal of my abortion, I think what a tremendous difference a single decision can make in one's life—and the lives of those around them. But, of course, all of us could say the same about any turn in the road our lives have taken.

Some Thoughts on Abortion and Birth Control

During that conversation with Uncle Wes in Phoenix, I also heard a surprising piece of information about my Grandmother Chamless. Uncle Wes said she told him she had undergone several abortions before her marriage to Grandpa. Since Uncle Wes and Grandma are both dead, I have no way of verifying his story. But I do remember Grandma saying to me when I was a young adult that "after I married your grandpa, I tried everything I could think of to keep from getting pregnant." But Grandpa was a fundamentalist preacher who didn't believe in birth control, let alone abortion, so although Grandma was 28 years old when they married, she bore him 11 children in the next 15 years. When she finally found the resources to leave him, I believe it was a great relief for her. Her sweet spirit endured until her death in her 80s, and while there is abundant evidence that she cherished every one of her children, I can't help thinking of her as a prisoner of her reproductive system. I'm very glad that birth control has come such a long way since my grandmother's day.

Grandma Chamless was perhaps exceptionally fertile, but she was far from being the only woman of her generation who was a prisoner of her reproductive system. My Grandma Rainbolt had eight children in 22 years, and there's some reason to believe that she would have had more, had she not nursed each baby as long as possible. Nursing mothers, it was believed, could not get pregnant, which is probably why a lot of mothers nursed their babies so long in those days. My mother told me that when her mother was pregnant with the last child, she was "madder than a wet hen." Even Grandpa was trying to comfort her. "I don't blame you for being upset, Ruth," Mom recalled hearing him say, "If I were in your place, I'd be kicking myself all around this house!"

Not all husbands were so sympathetic, though. My Grandma Rainbolt told me that when *her* mother was a midwife, there was one household where she always had to spend the night with a certain brand-new mother in order to keep the woman's husband from exercising his "matrimonial rights." I'm glad most husbands nowadays don't think of marriage as a license to commit rape, although apparently some still do.

While I think each child deserves two parents and it's a bad idea for girls to become mothers before they are mature adults, I'm glad there is considerably less social stigma now for unwed mothers and children born out of wedlock than when I was young. Today, girls who want to have their babies and keep them don't have to suffer the shame and emotional damage that unwed mothers did back then. But I wish there were more ways to educate them to the pitfalls of early pregnancy and the responsibilities of parenthood.

Recently, when I was talking about this book with a friend of mine who is almost 90 years old, she told me that her mother had died when she was eight. My friend didn't learn the cause of her mother's death, she said, until after she was grown, when an aunt told her that her mother had died from internal gangrene as the result of a botched abortion. When I told a mutual friend about this, she had a similar, less tragic, story to tell. This friend, who is about my age (I'll call her Carol), took her mother to the doctor when she was very old and in the early stages of Alzheimer's. In the course of his examination, the doctor asked Carol's mother how many times she had given birth. "One," she replied. But when he asked her how many times she had been pregnant, she surprised her daughter by saying, "Two—but I had an abortion with the other one." At first, Carol confessed, she thought her mother had lived a wild life in her youth, and she was just a little resentful that her mother had been so strict with her. But when she discovered that the abortion had come after her own birth, she speculated that it might have been for financial reasons. Around the time Carol and I were born, many families were still feeling the effects of the Great Depression, and most found it hard enough to feed the children they had, without adding more.

These examples and many others make me glad that birth control is so much more advanced than it was in those days, and that abortion is safe and legal in the United States—at least for now.

As for those who think abortion is murder, I can't see an embryo as a person any more than I can see a fertilized egg as a chicken or an acorn as an oak tree. And as for the few moments of physical pain a fetus may endure during an abortion, I don't believe it can compare to the accumulated physical and emotional pain even the happiest people experience over a lifetime. While life can be incredibly wonderful, it can also include a great deal of pain. For me, emotional pain has always been a lot harder to bear than physical pain, and I seriously doubt that a fetus can feel emotional pain. Nor can I believe that an aborted embryo or fetus is capable of anguishing over the lost opportunity of life.

Nevertheless, I don't take abortion lightly.

I am well aware of the "slippery slope" argument: If we accept abortion, what's to stop us from killing newborns, like the ancient Trojans or some modern Chinese are said to do with unwanted girl babies under the one-child rule? I believe the Supreme Court considered that and many other serious ethical questions in *Roe v. Wade* and came up with a humane and reasonable standard. Once human beings started practicing medicine, they took a tremendous number of the decisions regarding life and death out of the hands of God—or Nature, for those who don't believe in God. In consequence, we must use our intelligence to make ethical judgments about myriad issues regarding human life on a daily basis, and on this one I agree with the Court.

Having said all that, I can say unequivocally that I wish no woman ever had to face the decision of what to do about an unwanted or dangerous pregnancy. The decision to abort is not an easy one, and the emotional after-effects can be long lasting—especially if society stigmatizes abortion, as I know all too well. I have met more women than I can count who've had abortions, and I have never heard any of them say the experience was one they would have chosen if they could have avoided pregnancy in the first place. I have also known at least two mothers besides my own—both now dead—who were strongly opposed to abortion until their teenaged daughters became pregnant, whereupon they changed their minds. Yet social pressures are still so strong that many women—probably most women—who have abortions or who secure abortions for their teenage daughters are reluctant to admit it to anyone but their closest friends.

I am certain, though, that if abortion is murder, the world is awash in murderers and always has been. If all of these "murderers" were sent to prison or executed, there would be a whole lot more motherless children in this world. And, in my opinion, our world definitely doesn't need any more motherless children.

Many Thanks

Writing a memoir is tricky. Other people are involved, and some of them are integral parts of the story. So the first people I want to thank are my three daughters, Tamara, "Titi" and Julia, and their father, Harold, for encouraging my efforts to write my story without telling me how to write it. I think I am being totally objective in saying that they are, indeed, unique and wonderful people, and I hereby give them my permission to include me in their own stories, in which I may be seen in a very different light.

But there are many other people I have to thank:

First and foremost is Judith M. Kelly, who has prodded, pushed and encouraged me to write since the lucky day that we became friends after I moved to Oklahoma in 2003. She has been my muse and, on more than one occasion, even my patron. There is no way I can thank her enough.

My dear friend and former colleague from Oklahoma State University Professor Trish Macvaugh read several drafts and, in addition to giving much-appreciated encouragement, pointed out some typos. Professor Terry Werner, friend and former colleague at Harris-Stowe State University, volunteered to proof an early version of the manuscript, and Tripp Narup, my fellow reader from the Second Sunday Dinner Theatre, volunteered to proof the ante-antepenultimate draft. Any remaining typos and errors are the result of my compulsion to keep making changes long after I should have left the darn thing alone.

My fellow writers in the (Un)Stable Writers Group, Ben Moeller-Gaa, Amy Genova, Dawn Leslie Lenz, Autumn Rinaldi, Lisa Odak and Denise Mussman, have read portions of the book and given valuable feedback and encouragement.

My beautiful, multitalented niece, Patricia Chamless, volunteered to straighten out the formatting for me because I am technologically challenged. My youngest daughter, Julia, also volunteered to fix the formatting for me, but I turned her down because I knew she was stretched almost beyond the limit of endurance by her own writing and research efforts on a major headline-grabbing legal case that had been going on for more than two and a half years and is still in the courts as I write. But her offer touched my heart, as did daughter Tamara's frequent posts and emails containing tips on writing, publishing and finding agents. My middle daughter "Titi" has inspired me mainly by example with her very prolific and impressive record of publications and blogging.

Other dear friends who have read the manuscript in different stages and given encouragement are Sharon Wright, Helen Hudlin, Meg Rashbaum Selig, and Sue Cody.

Another former colleague at Harris-Stowe, Judith Repke, designed the beautiful cover. Working with Judy again brought back fond memories of those days when we collaborated on the president's reports, magazines, brochures, and flyers for the college.

Thanks, also, to friends who have encouraged my writing and given feedback on the cover design through Facebook: Carol A. Pettit, Shannon Kelly-Wilson, Marilyn Holt, Pamela Voisin, Judy Diaz, Susan Bullard, Anne Collins, Erica Nason, Jack E. Palmeri, Colin Vurek and my sons-in-law, Phillip Rieman and Brian Foley. If I have left anyone out, please let me know, and if the book sells enough to warrant paying for changes, I will add your name to the list.

I would be remiss if I did not thank all of the readers of my column in the Stillwater, Oklahoma, *NewsPress*. Two notables among that crowd are my dear friends Ed and Geri Whitehead. Your enthusiastic responses to my columns gave me the courage I needed to embark on a number of independent writing projects very late in life.

And many, many thanks to all of you who bought my first book, *The Dance of Life: Perspectives*. You gave me the courage to go on.

Discussion Questions
1. Have you or someone you know suffered from postpartum depression?
2. Do you know any mothers who have opted for abortions for their teenage daughters?
3. Do you think most women have had abortions are afraid to admit it publicly?
4. What would you have done if you had been in Pat's mother's place? Why?
5. Do you know anyone who gave up a baby at birth for adoption?
6. In your opinion, would Ronnie be a sex offender by today's standards? Should he be considered a sex offender?
7. What do you think of Pat's mother? Was she a victim, abuser, or both?
8. Can you relate to Pat's mother's situation as a professional woman in what was considered a man's field?
9. What do you think about the people who left the church over the scandal? What about those who stayed?
10. How do you feel about Pat's hearing before the presbyters? Should they have asked a young girl such intimate questions? Did they have a right to know about Pat's mother's sexual history before marriage?
11. Do you think Pat was wrong to lie to the presbyters?
12. How do you think the abortion and its consequences influenced Pat's emotional health and her subsequent relationships with men?
13. Looking at Pat's parents, who do you think was weak? Who was strong?
14. Can you relate to the relationship between Pat and her mother? Pat and her father?
15. Are there any surprises in the story?
16. Speaking of her mother, the author says, "I think her philosophy was that human failings should be hidden to avoid providing a bad example for others, whereas I have always believed that it's better

to know and deal with the truth, insofar as that's possible." Do you agree?
17. The author says, "I have come to the conclusion that while religion can make good people better, it can also make bad people worse. It's human nature, I think, to find in your religion the justification for being the kind of person you are already inclined to be." Do you agree?

Printed in Great Britain
by Amazon.co.uk, Ltd.,
Marston Gate.